Peoples and Cultures
of the World
Part I

Professor Edward F. Fischer

THE TEACHING COMPANY ®

PUBLISHED BY:

THE TEACHING COMPANY
4151 Lafayette Center Drive, Suite 100
Chantilly, Virginia 20151-1232
1-800-TEACH-12
Fax—703-378-3819
www.teach12.com

ISBN 1-56585-921-9

Edward F. Fischer, Ph.D.
Associate Professor of Anthropology, Vanderbilt University

Edward F. Fischer was educated at the University of Alabama at Birmingham and Tulane University, where he received his Ph.D. in anthropology in 1996. His research focuses on the modern Maya peoples of highland Guatemala and the ways that they have revitalized their culture as they have become integrated in the global economy.

Professor Fischer is the author of numerous professional articles and several books, including *Pan-Maya Activism in Guatemala* (co-edited with R. McKenna Brown), *Cultural Logics and Global Economies, Tecpán Guatemala: A Modern Maya Town in Local and Global Context* (co-authored with Carol Hendrickson), and *Pluralizing Ethnography* (co-edited with John Watanabe). He is currently studying Maya farmers who grow broccoli for export to the United States and working on a project comparing economic attitudes in Guatemala, Germany, and the United States.

Professor Fischer has received grants from the John D. and Catherine T. MacArthur Foundation, the Inter-American Foundation, the Wener-Grenn Foundation, and others. Since 1996, he has taught at Vanderbilt University, where he is Associate Professor of Anthropology and Director of the Center for Latin American and Iberian Studies. In 2002, he received the Jeffrey Nordhaus Award for Excellence in Teaching, and in 2004, he received the Ellen Gregg Ingalls Award for Excellence in Classroom Teaching.

Table of Contents
Peoples and Cultures of the World
Part I

Peoples and Cultures of the World

Scope:

What do we as humans share and what makes us different? What sorts of behavior are acceptable and what are not in different societies? What can this tell us about ourselves as human beings? This course addresses such questions by examining a wide range of cultural diversity. In looking at cultures around the world, we show how anthropology acts as a "mirror for humanity," teaching us about ourselves and about others.

Built around compelling examples of exotic customs, this course shows how cultures differ (from religious beliefs and marriage practices to political organization and economics) and addresses the question of why such differences exist and persist in the modern world. Studying cultural diversity also allows us to look at our own customs in a new light, and, in so doing, stimulates creativity.

We begin with a brief overview of the four subfields of anthropology: physical anthropology, archaeology, linguistics, and cultural anthropology. Physical anthropology defines our field of inquiry (what makes us biologically human) and shows how our evolutionary heritage continues to influence our actions. Archaeology gives us a sense of scale when speaking of societal trends and is increasingly meaningful for indigenous peoples seeking to reclaim their past.

The primary focus of the course is on modern cultures. To attempt to interpret other cultures, we must first understand language—not just the dictionary meanings of words (even if there were dictionaries of these languages) but the subtleties of communication. Sociolinguistics shows how dialect differences convey a great deal of cultural meaning; in English, for example, even women and men have distinct patterns of speaking that often lead to misunderstanding. Through such examples we will study the ways that language molds the very way we perceive and think about the world. This leads us to examine how mental models and pervasive metaphors (such as "time is money") shape our culture and how religion and magic fit into cultural schemes.

Having started at the level of language and thought—that is to say, with the individual—we move to how the individual fits into society through rites of passage and kinship relations. We focus particularly on the differences between matrilineal and patrilineal societies. This leads us to a discussion of marriage patterns (monogamous and polygamous) and the role of romantic love in societies that practice arranged marriages.

We then turn to an overview of cultures at different levels of social complexity, from bands and tribes to chiefdoms and states. We look to the subsistence strategies of gathering-and-hunting bands and horticulturist rainforest dwellers. We find that economic relations in these cultures are firmly embedded in social relations and that reciprocity and redistribution are the norm under certain circumstances. These societies also have different types of political organization, and we look at the problems of leadership in small-scale societies. We examine violence and warfare, as well as ways of keeping the peace.

Modern native cultures cannot be seen as isolated entities. Since the glory days of Western expansion, these cultures have come into increasing contact with the outside world. We look to some of the deadly misunderstandings that accompanied early European contact. We then turn to the expansion of capitalist economies. We find that the rational choice models of traditional economics do not hold up under cross-cultural comparison, and we review the attempts of economists and anthropologists to come to terms with cultural differences.

The course concludes with a discussion of how globalization has affected native peoples around the world in surprising ways, focusing particularly on the Maya of Guatemala and Mexico, where I have conducted my long-term ethnographic fieldwork. We examine the rise of global economies and how native ways of life have changed as a result. We also look to the resurgence of ethnic groups—and the potentials and pitfalls of a world increasingly divided along ethnic lines.

Lecture One
The Study of Humanity

Scope:

From the Greek *anthropos* and *logos*, anthropology is, quite literally, the study of humankind. And anthropologists take this broad mandate seriously. Other fields give us valuable insights into particular areas (for example, economics, history, or biology), but anthropology's genius is in looking at the interconnections among these spheres, bringing to bear the widest range of knowledge to understand the complexities and contradictions of the human condition.

In attempting a holistic perspective, anthropology spans the divide between science and humanity. Although we develop hypotheses and strive for scientific rigor in collecting data, the signature method of cultural anthropology (participant observation) is fundamentally subjective. Participant observation is going "there" (wherever "there" may be) and studying "them" (whomever "they" may be), living our lives as the natives live, if just for a year or two, so that we can contextualize the hard facts (from survey figures to caloric intake) with a subjective understanding of what their lives are like.

Outline

I. Cultural anthropology studies the range of human diversity found in the world and uses these data to address fundamental questions about human nature.

   A. Culture is learned.

   B. Despite how we often speak about them, cultures are not homogenous.

   C. The one great rule of culture is that it is always changing.

II. Anthropology is the study of humankind.

   A. Anthropology is one of the few academic disciplines that transcends the boundary between the sciences and the humanities.

   1. From the Greek, *anthropos* means "humanity" and *logos* means "writing about" or "the study of."

Anthropologists employ the tools of scientific research (testable hypotheses, random sampling, and so on) but also strive for more subjective understanding of the people we study.

   2. Max Weber distinguishes between *Verstehen* ("understanding") and *Erklärung* ("explanation"); anthropologists seek both *Verstehen* and *Erklärung*.

B. Rather than looking at just one aspect of the human condition, anthropology adopts a holistic approach.

   1. Economics, political science, psychology—these are all valuable disciplines. But alone, they each give us just part of the picture.

   2. Named for a famous Japanese film, the Rashomon effect describes the phenomenon of different people perceiving the same event in different ways.

   3. Anthropology looks at the interrelations between, for example, religion and economics, arguing that the human condition must be understood from a holistic perspective.

III. The discipline of anthropology is divided into four main subfields.

A. Biological anthropology looks at human evolution and modern biological variation.

B. Archaeology is the study of ancient civilizations and peoples, attempting to reconstruct past culture based on material remains.

C. Linguistics is the study of language and the many ways that humans communicate.

D. Cultural anthropology—called *social anthropology* in England—is the study of modern human traditions, customs, and worldviews.

IV. Despite its wide range of study, anthropology is united around a general perspective on humanity.

A. Anthropologists affirm that it is fundamentally important to study the range of human diversity, both past and present, in order to situate ourselves in the world.

B. By encouraging us to suspend our natural ethnocentrism, anthropology also provides an important way of understanding our own culture.

C. It is useful when talking about other cultures to distinguish between *emic* and *etic* perspectives. *Emic* is the view from within a culture; *etic* is the presumably more objective view of an outsider.

Readings:

Emily Schultz and Robert Lavenda, *Cultural Anthropology.*

Thomas Barfield, *The Dictionary of Anthropology.*

Gary Ferraro, *Classic Readings in Cultural Anthropology.*

Internet Resources:

http://anthro.palomar.edu/tutorials/cultural.htm.

Cultural Anthropology Tutorials. Dr. Dennis O'Neil, Palomar College.

Questions to Consider:

1. What is the difference between "objective" and "subjective" forms of understanding? How does anthropology attempt to reconcile the two?

2. How can different perspectives of the same event or phenomenon result in radically different memories—and what does this tell us about the limits of objectivity?

3. Can studying other cultures inspire creative thinking about our own society?

Lecture One—Transcript
The Study of Humanity

On Maundy Thursday, the Thursday before Easter in 1994, I was living in Tecpan Guatemala with my wife Maraika, who was pregnant with our first child. I was doing my doctoral dissertation fieldwork in cultural anthropology, which brought us to this predominantly Kaqchikel Maya town in the highlands of Guatemala. On this day we'd woken up early, as usual – one wakes up with the roosters in Tecpan – and fixed breakfast on our propane stove in the little two-room former schoolhouse where we lived. As we were washing dishes at the garden spigot that morning, one of our neighbors came by to give us a plate of sweet rolls.

We invited her in and served her coffee and served her some of the rolls, as is the custom in Tecpan, but we were somewhat surprised by this gift out of the blue, and then, not soon afterwards, the daughter of some other friends in town stopped by with another plate of the same sort of rolls, so we invited her in and began to quiz her on why the sudden gift of the sweet rolls. She explained everybody gave them to their neighbors and friends on Maundy Thursday. She just wasn't sure why; it's just what everyone did. After she left, we rushed to the bakery around the corner and bought the last few rolls and cookies that they had left. Back at home we scrambled to divide up our paltry offerings between all the many people who had opened their homes and their lives to us over the last months, trying to work out the intricate political calculus that has to go into such gifts, and a steady stream of friends dropped by the house delivering their *pan dulces*.

Trying to make too few rolls fit on too many plates, I got aggravated, aggravated first that I, the cultural anthropologist in town, had not known about this obviously important ritual, and then aggravated that my day's plans would be totally ruined as we would have to go around and deliver our embarrassingly small offerings to our friends, and then aggravated a bit by the senselessness of it all. We would be giving out gifts of about equivalent value to people who had earlier that day given us such gifts, and we ended up recycling lots of the rolls, and I suspect everybody else in town was doing the same thing that day. As we made our rounds, however, my aggravation gave way to delight, delight at getting to visit with our friends over coffee, delight at being able to symbolically reaffirm the bonds of friendship that were so important to us.

As I wrote up my field notes that night, I became embarrassed by my earlier aggravation. It wasn't very culturally sensitive of an anthropologist to be aggravated by such cultural customs, and as I wrote of the important role of such exchanges in maintaining community and culture in Tecpan, the way in which seemingly quirky or meaningless customs make sense, not only make sense but appear indispensable when they're understood in their full cultural context, and I marveled at how the exceedingly intricate and elusive social fabric of Tecpan was publicly revealed and fortified that day in the exchange of sweet rolls.

So in this course, we'll be looking at cultures around the world and attempting to explain why they do the things that often seem to us to be odd, or exotic, or even sometimes repulsive. Our goal is going to be twofold: first, to expose you to other cultures and other ways of doing things, to give you an overview of the extent of human diversity and cultural diversity in the world. This may range from the quirky – why do we have traffic lights in the United States that go green, yellow, red? Why don't we have traffic lights that go red, yellow, and green? Why do we call our mother's sister's son cousin? It's just the way it is, but in many societies around the world, mother's sister's children would be called by a different kinship name than father's sister's children, for example, both of which we call cousins. It's going to range from quirky elements such as this to more profound elements. What does it mean to be a man, or what does it mean to be a woman? What's the meaning of death? Is rationality a human universal? And what do we as humans share and what makes us different? What can this tell us about ourselves as human beings and about human nature?

Anthropology, like philosophy, touches on these fundamental questions of being, but anthropology does so in a very grounded way, relying not on hypothetical situations, or on musings, but rather on the data of fieldwork, our observations about what people actually do, what people think, how they act in the world. In addressing these larger issues, the second aim of this class is to turn the anthropological lens on our own culture, our own ways of doing things, making anthropology, in the words of the anthropologist Alfred Krober, a mirror for humanity.

By studying other cultures and other customs, other belief systems, I hope to make you question some of your own assumptions about what is natural, what's human nature, what just is, and it's my belief that in doing so we can provoke new and creative perspectives on our own lives. I think that the study of other cultures is inherently interesting. Of course, I'm partisan, I'm a cultural anthropologist, but it has something valuable to offer all of us as members of our own societies. It's a privilege for me to be able to share with you my passion for anthropology, and I trust that you will find it worthwhile as well.

When you hear the word anthropology, what probably comes to mind is an Indiana Jones-like figure, dressed in khakis and a pith helmet, chopping his way through the jungle in search of hidden treasures and temples; or perhaps you think of scientists studying human evolution, piecing together early hominid skeletons such as Lucy or digging them up in East Africa; or maybe you think of anthropologists as going to study faraway locations, to study exotic peoples. In fact, we do all of these things. I'm a cultural anthropologist—I study living peoples, living cultures—although I work alongside archaeologists, biological anthropologists, and linguists. Cultural anthropology, as the name implies, is the study of modern cultures. Through cultural anthropology, we intend to explain variation and document alternative ways of life.

The word culture comes to us from the Latin root, the same root as cultivate and agriculture, and this sense of cultivate gives rise to its usage as a synonym for high culture. We often think of culture as being the opera, ballet, art, the sorts of things that cultivated people can appreciate. But culture also has this more democratic modern usage, recognizing that everyone has culture and that we all have different sorts of culture. Multiculturalism has become a catchphrase of the day. I'm going to save a more detailed discussion of the culture concept for a later lecture; but since we're going to be using the term so frequently, it deserves defining it now.

We can define culture as the learned behaviors, the ways of looking at the world, worldviews that are shared by a variably defined group of people, a culture group. Culture encompasses symbols and beliefs as well as behavior and things. It's important to remember that the distribution of any one trait within a group is variable; cultures are not internally homogenous. Think of our own culture, think of how diverse U.S. society is, and yet there are discernible overall patterns. We can speak of various levels of culture: national culture, regional culture, various sorts of subcultures based around music or sports or sexual identity or other interests. I'm a member of an academic culture, I'm a member of my campus culture, I'm a member of my neighborhood culture, of Southern culture, of U.S. culture. We each belong to a multitude of different kinds of identity groups and ever more so in this age of globalization.

In this sense, we all juggle multiple identities that we can call on, identities that we improvise on in particular contexts, and this is really the art of living socially. It's too easy to think of culture as simply being this strict category. There's always a lot of eternal diversity within cultures. We allow this for our own culture, and, as we're going to see in this class, we have to allow for other cultures as well. Not all Mayan people are alike, not all Germans are alike, not all Kayapo people are alike, and we're going to focus on some of this diversity in the class. It also bears emphasizing at this point that culture is something that we improvise on. It's models that we hold in our minds, but we're not cultural automatons. We improvise on the cultural schemes that we get through socialization.

There are few cultural universals; there are very few cultural universals in the world. Every culture recognizes different genders; that's a cultural universal. Every culture has language, every culture interestingly enough plays games, but these cultural universals are so broad as to tell us very little about what makes us human. Every culture has a moral code, for example, but what that moral code is varies significantly from society to society. The one great rule of culture is that it's always changing. Indeed, some would argue that it's misleading to speak of culture as a thing, to use it as a noun. In many ways, it's better conceived of as an ongoing process, something, as I've said before, that we're constantly improvising. The anthropologist Arjun Appadurai argues that the term should only be used in its adjectival form—cultural elements, cultural beliefs, cultural practices—and in doing so avoids any implication of stasis or boundedness. Culture's not a thing; it's a process, it's a dynamic process that is changing all the time.

To back up a bit, what is anthropology? We've defined culture. But what is anthropology? if we're going to be studying cultural anthropology. Anthropology comes from Greek roots, and it's most basically defined as the study of humanity. *Anthropos* is the Greek root for man, really mankind or humanity. There was another Greek root for the gender male *Anga* but *anthropos* is man, humanity. *Ology* implies science, the study of, coming from the Greek word logos, for word. Thus we can define anthropology as the science of man or, rather, the science of humanity. But interestingly enough, *logos* can also be translated not as just the study of or the science of but also as discourse. In fact, *logos*, with implications of logic and scientific rigor, was not distinguished from *mythos* until the work of Pythagoras and the other scholars in the 6th century B.C. Before that, the discourse of logos referred to myth as well as science, and even to gossip as well.

This leads us to an alternate meaningful definition of anthropology, the bearer of tales, or the bearer of scandals or the bearer of gossip, which is what we as cultural anthropologists really do. We bring back stories from the field, stories of other people's lives, stories and legends that they tell, and we bring back and we represent—and I use represents here in a dual meaning—we represent these elements to our audience here in the States, and we use them as representatives of larger social truths. We bring stories back and we represent these stores to our audiences here and we hopefully use them to illustrate larger truths about social processes and about the human condition. Clifford Geertz, an anthropologist who works at the Institute for Advanced Study in Princeton, in a very influential 1973 book titled *The Interpretation of Cultures*, gives us a very useful definition of culture. He says, "Believing with Max Weber (a famous German sociologist), believing with Max Weber that man is an animal, suspended in webs of significance he himself has spun, I take culture to be those webs and the analysis of it, therefore, not to be an experimental science in search of law but an interpretive one in search of meanings."

These alternate definitions—Is anthropology a science? Is it the science of humanity or is it an interpretive endeavor, the bearer of tales? Is it a discourse-based discipline?—these alternate definitions reflect a growing division within anthropology between scientists and humanists. Some anthropology departments have even split up.

Most famously, Stanford has two separate departments: a department of anthropological sciences and a department of cultural anthropology. Despite this divide, what we as anthropologists really do best is travel these divisions. We anthropologists argue that no one perspective has a monopoly on the truth and thus we should avail ourselves of all the analytic resources available, be they science or not, or discourse on humanities.

In practice, anthropologists are generally a little of both, a little bit scientist, a little bit humanist. We certainly gather data; we're much concerned with the reliability of the data that we collect. We develop hypotheses and theories, we test these based on fieldwork and data collection, and yet at the same time we mold these data into stories, representing our findings in a way that's meaningful for our contemporary audiences. The German sociologist Max Weber made a useful distinction between *verstenen*, understanding, more subjective comprehension, and *erklarung*, clarification, explanation, the nuts and bolts of how something works. Based on this distinction what anthropologists try and do really is to capture both *verstenen*, the subjective sense of the experience, and *erklarung*, the scientific explanation for why things are the way they are.

Anthropology, in contrast to the other theologies—biology, sociology, ecology, psychology—anthropology looks at not one aspect of the human condition but at the interconnectedness of all aspects of humanness. Economists study the economic life of humans, psychologists study the psychology, sociologists the social aspect, and these are all very important disciplines and they have a lot to teach us. Indeed, we as anthropologists frequently poach the insights of biology, of economics and psychology, as we will see in the course of these series of lectures. But anthropology is a very ecumenical discipline and this is really what attracted me to it in the first place. Anthropology sees that what gets lost in such particular perspectives, such disciplinary perspectives, is the interconnectedness of it all, of life, of the human condition.

One aspect of human behavior is influenced by and influences other spheres. We know this instinctively in a way. Politics is tied to religion, economics is tied to psychology, biology is tied to social organization, and this is all tied together with the glue of culture. Again, this is something that we intuitively recognize, I think. One's religion affects the way in which one votes, for example. Politics affects religion; religion affects politics. I was reading not long ago actually that church attendance is a better indicator of party affiliation in the United States than income is. But, anyway, this is something that we as academics can easily forget, the interrelatedness of it all, as we work away in our increasingly narrow perspectives and specializations. Thus a basic tenet of anthropology is its holistic approach, looking at the whole of the human condition and not just one aspect.

In some ways this is akin to Gestalt psychology, gestalt analysis, the school of psychology that interprets phenomena as organized wholes rather than as aggregates of distinct parts, maintaining that the whole is greater than the sum of its parts. Most phenomena, material and social, are simply too complex to be fully understood by looking at just one variable, from being approached from just one angle.

There's an effect we call in anthropology the Rashomon effect, and this comes from, is named for, the classic 1950 Japanese film that looks at a rape outside the city gates of a Japanese city from four different and four contradictory points of view: from the point of view of the victim; from the point of view of a policeman; from the point of view of an observer; from the point of view of the perpetrator—the same objective event, but it gets interpreted in very different ways. In anthropology we say nobody has a hold on the truth. It's good for outside observers and anthropologists to come in and have one perspective, also to record the perspective of cultural insiders, and by combining multiple perspectives, by looking at the same phenomenon from different angles, we get a much richer, a much more complex, a much deeper understanding of the phenomena we're trying to describe.

Using the broadest definition, anthropology is the study of humanity, the study of people, and under this definition we're all practicing anthropologists, not just those of us who have Ph.D.s in the field. We're all practicing anthropologists; we all constantly analyze the world around us. We try and divine the motivations of others and act accordingly. It's our very nature to try and understand the social world around us and thus to be anthropologists. When friends ask how much I work, I tell them I'm working all the time; I'm working right now, studying you, studying human behavior, human interaction. Sometimes studying anthropology can be a burden. It can make one hyperaware of social situations, too aware for one's own good, if that is indeed possible. We're going to give a lecture later on in the series about gift-giving, and I often have students come up to me and say "You know, that lecture you gave on gift giving, it's made me think about giving gifts way too much ever since then," and it can really paralyze people in some ways to know too much about why we do what we do.

Interdisciplinarity is very much in vogue in the academy these days, partly as a reaction to the hyperspecialization of academic fields. Anthropology was interdisciplinary long before it was cool. This is the very basis of the discipline, to look at human behavior and the interconnections of different aspects of human behavior, and why should we be constrained by disciplinary boundaries, which are themselves just historical artifacts of the time when knowledge seemed much more containable. American anthropology is generally divided into four subfields, and these are: biological anthropology, which looks at human behavior and modern biological variation; archaeology, the study of ancient civilizations and peoples, attempting to reconstruct past cultures based on material remains; linguistics, the study of language and the many ways humans communicate, both verbally and nonverbally; and, finally, cultural anthropology, which is often called social anthropology in England and at Harvard, which is the study of modern human traditions, customs, and worldviews.

The structure of this course follows an expanding concentric circle to examine human culture. In the first part of the course, we're going to begin by looking at what makes us human, the role of culture and biology in human behavior, the influence of language on thought and thus culture. We see, for example, how men's speech differs from women's speech in modern U.S. society. We look at the cultural misunderstandings that can ensue from dialectical differences, and we look at how certain cultural metaphors such as "time is money" can mold our views of the world. In the second part of the class, we move out from the individual's relationship with culture to look at the basic social forms that hold communities and societies together. We're going to look at the role of rites of passage as marking stages in people's lives. We're going to look at how kinship ties and religion can bind people together. We'll learn about the Trobriand

Islanders of Melanesia, a matrilineal society where descent is traced through female lines and yet where formal positions of power are held by men. We're going to study the Fulbe of northern Cameroon and their unique blending of Islam and indigenous traditions of magic and sorcery.

In the third section of the class, we're going to turn to cultural patterns of societies at different levels of complexity, and we're going to follow a typology of bands, tribes, chiefdoms, and states. We're going to examine, for example, the Dobe Ju/'hoansi of Botswana and Namibia, nomadic gatherers and hunters who have no chiefs or permanent political leaders and who have very little conception of private property. We're going to see how family ties and reciprocal bonds hold society together in such circumstances. We then contrast this with the political structure of groups such as the Yanamamu, who find themselves in frequent conflict and at war with neighboring groups. The Yanamamu exemplify some of the more exotic customs that we're going to examine in this class, but keep in mind, exotic from our perspective. Exotic is always relative; customs are very rarely exotic if ever for the people who are practicing them. But the Yanomamo, they practice cannibalism. They have shamans who ingest hallucinogenic snuff to contact the spirit world. Their headmen often have several wives.

Modern native cultures cannot be seen as isolated entities. Since the glory days of Western expansion, they've come into increasing contact with the outside world, so we're going to look at some of the deadly misunderstandings that accompanied early European contact and try and explain the death of Captain Cook at the hand of Hawaiians in 1779. We're going to turn to the expansion of capitalist economies and look at rational choice models of traditional economics and how these don't hold up in many ways under cross-cultural comparison. We're going to review the attempts of economists and anthropologists to come to terms with cultural differences, and we're going to look at contemporary U.S. culture and the bases of our own economic system, and the symbols and identities that have become highly marketable commodities in this age of late capitalism.

We're going to conclude the course by looking at how globalization has affected native peoples around the world in surprising ways, including the erosion of traditional life ways and the simultaneous resurgence of ethnic groups. Here we're going to focus particularly on the Maya in Guatemala and Mexico, where I've conducted most of my own long-term ethnographic fieldwork. My early work focused on the Mayan cultural activists in Guatemala and their fight for civil rights. My more recent work looks at how Mayan peoples fit into the global modern economy. You might be surprised, for example, to learn that a fair percentage of the broccoli in this country is grown by small holding Mayan farmers in the Guatemalan highlands; and as we're going to see in a later lecture, our vegetable consumption in the U.S. has hidden impacts on native people, such as the Maya, in faraway locations.

There's a pronounced romantic tradition in anthropology; I think it's the allure of the foreign and the exotic that pulls us toward the discipline in the first place, but in the process of doing fieldwork we anthropologists move beyond such shallow romanticization to give a more intimate, a richer, a more complex understanding of the people that we study. In studying such societies, you'll be asked to suspend your natural ethnocentrism. Ethnocentrism is the belief that your culture's way of doing things is the only or the best way of doing things. This can be difficult. We're going to discuss customs that you may find odd or even repulsive: cannibalism, ritualized homosexuality, domestic violence. But before we can pronounce moral judgment, we must fully understand the context in which these customs operate.

Often, what appearss to us to be exotic or even bizarre is seen to make perfect sense within the cultural context in which we find it. Here we can distinguish between emic and etic views of the world. An emic perspective is a cultural insider's view of how things are; an etic perspective is an outsider's view, and what we're doing in anthropology is combine an outsider's perspective, an etic perspective on culture, with an insider's view, an emic perspective on culture, and in combining those the idea is that we can get at a richer understanding of human behavior.

In the beginning of this lecture, I mentioned that my wife was pregnant with our son while we were living in Tecpan in 1994. We went back to Germany, where my wife is from, for the birth, but during the pregnancy in Tecpan we employed the services of

Anjelina, a woman widely considered to be the best midwife in Tecpan. Anjelina's mother was a midwife, as was her mother's mother. She suspects the tradition goes back even farther, although she can't say for sure. Anjelina is a trained nurse as well as a traditionalist midwife, and she's able to perform ritual sweat bath therapies which involve herbal massages and prayers to Mayan and Catholic gods and offerings, as well as refer us to the regional hospital for ultrasounds if she thinks we need it.

We became very close to Anjelina and her family during our stay, and I've always respected the way that she's able to manage these diverse and sometimes contradictory cultural identities. Anjelina herself was pregnant at the time, and she delivered her girl a few months after my son was born. Estefani, her young girl, is a precocious, somewhat spoiled, child, the youngest of four sisters. In addition to midwifery, Anjelina sells hand woven blouses and skirts, the colorful dress that you probably associate with Mayan peoples, and she often dresses her daughter Estefani exceptionally well.

I was surprised to find out during a recent visit to Tecpan a few years ago that Estefani was very much infatuated with Pikachu and Pokemon and all of these other Japanese animated characters. I found it ironic that this young Kaqchikel speaking, traditional dress wearing girl was taken with the not quite latest thing in global pop culture. In fact, I used a photo of Estefani holding a Pikachu balloon while decked out in her finest traditional dress on the cover of a recent book, but I've come to realize in looking at this photo over and over again that the irony that I see in Estefani's fascination with Pikachu is my irony; and it's not Estefani's and it's not her parents'. Estefani and her parents see nothing ironic about being Maya and being modern at the same time. They're just trying to live their lives as best as they can given the circumstances, and, as we'll see in the lectures to come, native peoples around the world find themselves in similar circumstances. In this course, we're going to go beyond these ironies to discover the more profound lessons we have to learn from the Maya, from the Trobriand Islanders, from the Fulbe, from the Dobe Ju/'hoansi and from other indigenous peoples.

Lecture Two
The Four Fields of Anthropology

Scope:

Anthropology comprises four broad subfields: biological anthropology, archaeology, linguistics, and cultural anthropology. This course focuses on cultural diversity and human commonalities around the world, but we cannot study culture in isolation. Thus, in this lecture, we look to biological anthropology and the study of early humans to discover what makes our remarkable species unique—from big brains and language to opposable thumbs and bipedalism. In a similar vein, we turn to archaeology for lessons from the past about the rise and fall of civilizations, trying to understand the present in terms of the distant past. Much of what we know about other cultures comes to us through interviews; thus, an understanding of language and linguistics allows us to interpret what we learn in the field.

Today, biological anthropologists, archaeologists, and linguists are turning their talents to a number of unconventional uses. Forensic anthropologists, for example, work with the FBI to reconstruct crime scenes and determine causes of death in badly decomposed remains. Archaeologists have excavated garbage dumps to help large cities better understand where waste comes from (with unexpected results). Linguists, working with archaeologists and others, have created signs to mark nuclear waste dumps that are designed to be readable in 10,000 years.

Outline

I.   Biological anthropology studies the physical adaptations of humans to their environment; we look to biological anthropology to define what it means to be human.

   A. *Homo sapiens* first arose some 200,000 years ago in the savannas of east Africa.

   B. A small number of very important features make modern humans biologically unique.

1. Humans possess opposable thumbs, which allows for tool use, and walk bidepally, which frees the hands for other tasks.
2. Humans have large brains, which, in turn, allows for the development of both language and culture.
3. Humans practice a "K" strategy of reproduction, meaning we have very few offspring but care for them intensely.
4. Culture has allowed humans to opt out of many of the environmental pressures of natural selection.

C. *Race* is a loaded term and one that biological anthropologists generally avoid.
1. Genetic variation is greater within human races than between them, although interracial differences are especially evident in skin color, facial proportions, and similar characteristics.
2. Thus, race is not very useful as a biological category, although it remains an important social category.

D. Biological anthropology has branched out in recent years to include not only the study of early human evolution and human variation but also the burgeoning field of forensic anthropology.

II. Archaeology is the study of ancient cultures through their material remains.

A. Archaeology can teach us lessons from the past about the rise and fall of civilizations and the histories that go unrecorded in the history books.

B. Archaeologists employ a number of methods.
1. The most basic is "dirt archaeology"—digging up the remains of ancient societies. Archaeologists are often hindered by the scarcity of remains.
2. Archaeologists have turned to new technologies, including satellite imagery, mass spectrometry, and isotope isolation analyses.

C. In addition to traditional archaeology, some researchers have used their methods to study uncommon subjects, such as the archaeology of modern U.S. garbage dumps.

III. Linguistics is the study of human language.

 A. Anthropological linguists are concerned with understanding how people actually speak, or descriptive linguistics. In contrast, prescriptive linguistics seeks to set standards for how people *should* speak.

 B. Sociolinguistics is the study of language use and social meanings and holds the most importance for cultural anthropology.

 C. Linguists have begun to pursue a number of unusual applications for their research, including artificial intelligence, marketing, and monument design.

IV. Cultural anthropology examines social structures (legal, economic, and civil systems), as well as the more ephemeral cultural glue that holds them together.

 A. Culture provides a template for behavior rather than strictly prescribing actions.

 B. Culture is shared but is not perfectly distributed among any given population.

 C. In recent years, cultural anthropologists have turned their attentions toward their own cultures, and a number now work in marketing and design, among other nontraditional venues.

Readings:

Brian Fagan, *People of the Earth: An Introduction to World Prehistory*.

William Rathje, *Rubbish! The Archaeology of Garbage*.

Michael Brown, *The Search for Eve*.

Bill Bass and Jon Jefferson, *Death's Acre: Inside the Legendary Forensic Lab-- the Body Farm--Where the Dead Do Tell Tales*.

Internet Resources:

http://anthro.palomar.edu/tutorials/physical.htm.

Physical Anthropology Tutorials. Dr. Dennis O'Neil, Palomar College.

Questions to Consider:

1. What makes humans biologically unique? What could have been the evolutionary pressures that resulted in bipedalism and big brains?

2. What is race—biologically and culturally? Why is it such an important social category?

3. What can the study of ancient societies teach us about our own culture?

Lecture Two—Transcript
The Four Fields of Anthropology

Anthropology has the grand goal of studying all of humanity; anything related to the human condition is fair game for anthropologists to study, and this is an incredibly liberating scope and an incredibly intimidating mandate. Of course, human behavior is too complex to study using a unified overarching paradigm, such as we find in physics or chemistry or biology, and, as a result, anthropology is a very diverse field. We break down the discipline into four main subfields, and those are: biological anthropology; archaeology; linguistics; and cultural anthropology. Each of these subfields has its own set of subfields and is increasingly specialized; yet the benefit of working under the umbrella of anthropology is that we have the intellectual freedom to cross over these boundaries. In the lecture today, we'll review these four subfields, focusing on how they link together to help us understand and define modern human cultures.

What makes us human? If humanity is our subject, then what is it that defines it? To answer this foundational question, we have to turn to biological anthropology. Actually, when I was in school, this was called physical anthropology, but today so many anthropologists are using genetic research that we've redefined it as biological anthropology. Biological anthropology is concerned with the evolution of the human species, with the behavior of nonhuman primates, and with biological variation between human populations. Let me say a couple of words about evolution. It's a common misconception, first of all, that Darwin invented evolution. Evolution was an idea very much in the air at the time in the mid-19th century, linked with notions of the inevitability of progress. This was, after all, the age of industrialization, and dramatic social, political, and technological changes were occurring in the world.

In fact, as we all know, Darwin only published his results when it looked like Alfred Wallace was going to trump his findings, and so it was in 1859 that Darwin published *On the Origin of Species by Means of Natural Selection, or the Preservation of Favorite Races in the Struggle for Existence*. Darwin didn't invent evolution, but he gave us the mechanism for how evolution works, and that is natural selection. Darwin's notion of natural selection or the struggle for existence states that under natural competition, favorable traits will allow certain individuals to be more successful, and this means to have more offspring and thus pass these favorable traits on in greater frequencies to the next generation. Over time, and this can be hundreds of years or thousands of years, maybe even tens of thousands of years, if these traits offer enough reproductive benefits, they may become the norm for a population.

As a sideline, I would mention here that Stephen J. Gould has made his career critiquing Darwin's gradual evolution, and Gould says that actually what we find is punctuated equilibrium, periods of rapid evolutionary change followed by periods of stability and then punctuated once again with rapid evolutionary change. This seems to suit the facts of human evolution better than Darwin's theory in some ways. But Darwin's theory of natural selection gives us the classic definition for evolution: descent with modification enacted through natural selection. Darwin didn't know what caused the variation; we now know that it's caused by genetic mutations and recombination, but he gave us the mechanism through which it works.

The evolutionary history of humans is relatively brief in the big scheme of things. The earth is over 5 billion years old, and modern humans only came along about 200,000 years ago. The hominid line, and this is humanlike apes, of which humans are the only extant species, the hominid line probably broke off about 5 million years ago, and the earliest best examples we have are of the Australopithecines such as Lucy, famous Lucy, which was found in 1974 by Donald Johansson in Ethiopia. Lucy and the Australopithecines evolved into Homo habilus, the first humans to use tools, or the first hominids to use tools, about 2.5 million years ago, which evolved into Homo erectus about 1.7 million years ago and finally Homo sapiens around 200,000 years ago, a drop in the bucket in the big evolutionary scheme of things.

What sets us apart biologically as human beings are the combination of three key traits: opposable thumbs; bipedalism, that we walk on two legs; and having these huge big brains. Alone, these don't distinguish us from our closest living primate relatives. All primates, for example, have opposable thumbs. I was at the zoo recently and I looked at the gorillas, and the gorillas have these incredibly opposed toes as well, big toes so that they can use their feet as they would their hands. Opposable thumbs, the benefit of them is that it allows for more precise tool use, and tool use has been seen as being a distinctly human trait, although some recent studies of chimp population show that chimps can sometimes use tools as well.

For example, they've been observed in the wild going out, and they'll break off a branch of a tree, take off all of the leaves, and then carry that branch around for a period of time, and then when they run across a termite mound or an ant hill they'll stick the branch down in there and let the termites or ants crawl up the branch and then pull it out and eat it like a lollipop or a Popsicle. They also, chimpanzees, will sometimes pick leaves and chew them and make them into a little bundle and then soak up water in the crevices of trees and then squeeze it into their mouths. Granted, these aren't the most sophisticated tools in the world, but crucially they indicate foresight, breaking off a branch of a tree and carrying it around for a while and then sticking it in a termite mound. They're tools; it's tool usage, taking an item from nature, modifying it for a different purpose, and then using it later.

Opposable thumbs, even opposable thumbs that use tools, don't distinguish us from chimpanzees. But combined with bipedalism, walking on two legs, this really sets hominids and the hominid branch apart from the rest of our primate relatives. It's still something of a mystery why there was a switch to bipedalism because it seems there are all sorts of drawbacks to walking on two legs. We have severe lower back problems, we have knee problems, we have ankle problems, but it did free up our hands for tool use and for transportation. But the tool use and the bipedalism really come together when brains start getting larger, and this was late. This was very late in human evolution, long after bipedalism appeared. Lucy and the other Australopithecines, they were bipedal, they had opposable thumbs, they probably used tools, but they had brains the size of chimpanzees.

It's not until we get into Homo sapiens that we get these ungainly large brains, but it was the increase in brain size that allowed us to develop language and thus to develop culture, but it brought problems as well. Big-brained babies are hard to give birth to, and, in fact, the human female's pelvic size and shape are a compromise between having as large of a birth canal opening as possible and still being able to walk upright. And as large as human babies' brains are at birth, they don't stop there. Humans have this sustained period of postnatal brain growth and development. This is why nutrition and intellectual stimulation are so crucial in the first years of life.

Biologists distinguish between different types of reproductive strategies, and there's a continuum their ranges from R—that stands for the rate of reproduction—to K. K stands for carrying capacity (K, carrying capacity, go figure) but it's a continuum. R-selected species have lots of offspring, and they don't invest a lot of time in them, but they offset the higher mortality rate for their offspring by high absolute numbers, and here we can think of all the insects, mice, rats, roaches; even cats and dogs are more R selected, have more offspring than humans do. K-selected species, on the other hand, have fewer offspring and invest very heavily in the offspring they do have, making sure that they survive to reach reproductive age themselves. Having helpless infants with these big brains may well have led—and humans are the most K-selected species of all, and having helpless infants with these big brains may have well led to pair-bonding between parents to care for their children and thus the early foundations of society as a whole.

Big brains allow us the capacity for language and thus the capacity for culture, and big brains and language and culture changes everything. It changes the very rules of the evolutionary game for humans. We can change our environment rather than be changed by it. Look at cities like Phoenix or Tucson, these huge cities in the middle of the desert with manicured lawns and even golf courses outside. It's a remarkable feat of human engineering that we can live in such environments. The National Science Foundation maintains a research station in the Arctic Circle. We can live anywhere as human beings now, but we remain biological beings, and, given this, our ultimate mandate is to go forth and multiply, to reproduce ourselves. But here again, culture has been able to short-circuit the pleasure mechanism that allows us to reproduce ourselves; with birth control, for example, we can have the gratification without the reproductive consequences.

Let me say a word or two here about race. We're all Homo sapiens; this is the first and most important thing. We're all Homo sapiens, and at the genetic level racial categorizations are all but meaningless.

There's greater genetic variation within races than between races. Granted, the variation that does exist produces very visible features—skin color, the shape of the face, the shape of the eyes, the shape of the nose, and so forth—and we often use these physical traits as a shorthand for cultural patterns. Race is an important social category but not a very important biological category.

What do anthropologists do, biological anthropologists? They study human evolution, and probably the most famous images we have of biological anthropologists are paleoanthropologists such as Richard Leakey and his family digging up fossils in the deserts of east Africa. Physical anthropologists also work as primatologists, showing how our close relatives might shed light on human evolution. Researchers, such as Jane Goodall working with chimps or Dian Fosse with gorillas, conduct almost cultural studies of these primate populations, and, if you've seen any of the films in this genre, you realize just how human gorillas and chimps can be (or perhaps just how gorilla and chimp-like humans can be). But physical anthropologists are also turning their attention to new areas of research, and foremost among these, the fastest growing field in anthropology, is probably forensic anthropology, using the techniques developed to study ancient human skeletal remains to solve modern crimes.

Police departments, the FBI, will call in physical anthropologists to help sex and date skeletons that they found—for example, reconstruct victims' facial and body appearances. Most famously, the anthropologist Bill Bass, who works at the University of Tennessee, runs what is called the Body Farm, and this was made famous by a Patricia Cornwell novel of the same name. There, he and his colleagues, his graduate students and colleagues place donated human corpses in different sorts of contexts. They'll put them under water, they'll bury them three feet deep, they'll bury them six feet deep, they'll put them in a tin shed, or in the trunk of a car, and then they document the decomposition of the human bodies, the levels of gases, the amino acid breakdowns, the life cycle of maggots that grow in human remains, and these data can then be used to help police departments determine the time of death, post-mortem circumstances, and so forth.

Let me turn to archaeology. Archaeology, we're all familiar with archaeology; archaeology looks at the material remains of past cultures, attempting to understand those cultures through their artifacts. This is no small task, trying to reconstruct a civilization basically based on their garbage, on their trash, and this requires a lot of imagination. Archaeologists are able to document the processes of plant and animal domestication, of urbanization, of the rise and fall of civilizations. They ask the big picture questions. What caused the fall of Rome? Why did Mayan civilization collapse? Was it warfare? Was it environmental degradation? Was it climatic change? To think that we have nothing to learn from ancient cultures is just hubris; just as statesman and diplomats these days still study the Peloponnesian wars, it's good for us to learn the lessons of ancient civilizations that flourished and then failed.

Archaeologists employ a number of different methods; the most basic is dirt archaeology, literally going up and digging up the remains of ancient civilizations. In recent years, technological advances have really changed the nature of archaeology. We can use satellite images to identify new sites; we use mass spectrometry to allow us to source obsidian and clay and reconstruct trade routes. Working with biological anthropologists, archaeologists are using isotope isolation analysis to uncover the diets of ancient populations from their skeletal remains. This is all remarkable stuff, a whole new world of information opened up by these technological changes.

But, as archaeologists are gaining a sharper image of the past, they're also increasingly engaging modern indigenous populations. My colleague Arthur Demarest, who works in the Maya area, is a great example of this. He made his name discovering ancient Mayan cities; he's been called the real Indiana Jones, and right now he's working at the ancient Mayan city-state of Conquin. As part of the project, he started involving the local communities of Mayan Indians who live in the area, and this started simply, first giving soccer uniforms to the local team, donating a mill, or helping them build a well. But this has gradually evolved into a more holistic plan for the development of the area, and this is an area of extreme poverty, so the archaeologists are working to help set up health clinics, community pharmacies, even promote eco-tourism in the area.

Demarest and these archaeologists got involved because this is just the right thing to do. People were literally dying of hunger outside of their archaeological camp; they had to do something, but it turns out it's good archaeology as well. It makes these local Mayan populations feel vested in the archaeological site; they feel like it's theirs in some meaningful way, and so they protect it from looters, and they see the value in archaeology, especially since it promotes tourism, and it even rekindles a sense of ethnic pride.

Another interesting thing that archaeologists have been doing lately, and this is also another Mayan archaeologist, William Rathje at the University of Arizona. He runs what's called the most unconventional archaeology project in the world, and it's called the Garbage Project, and it's been going on since 1973. Rathje began in Tucson, where he did archaeological methods, laying out a grid, recording the stratigraphy, digging trenches, all of the things that we associate with archaeologists; he did this in the garbage dump in Tucson, and what he found was surprising, especially given the prevailing wisdom of the burgeoning environmental movement at the time. The bad guys, if you'll remember, in the early mid-70s were fast food packaging and disposable diapers, and it turned out, based on Rathje's archaeology, that these don't take up very much space in the dumps. Fast food packaging only accounted for about 0.5% in weight and 0.3% in volume, diapers only 1% in weight and 1.4% in volume.

What was it? There was something that provided clear stratographic layers for Rathje that could mark every year, year in and year out. What it was, was paper products, newspapers, but more than that telephone books, a clear stratographic layer for every year of yellow and white pages. Rathje has gone on to do similar sorts of work in other cities around the world—New Orleans, Milwaukee, Mexico City, even Sydney, Australia—and he's expanded out the scope of his work, not only looking at environmental implications of garbage dumps but looking at diets. For example, it turns out that people, when they self-report what they're eating, often idealize their diet. If you go back and look at their garbage, you see all the Twinkie wrappers in the vegetarian household's garbage and so forth, so we see what's really going on rather than what people say is going on.

Linguistics looks at the different forms of communication, variation among human languages, and how thoughts are developed within the mind. Let me make a clear distinction here; most anthropological linguists are descriptive linguists, and we contrast this with prescriptive linguists. Descriptive linguists try and describe how people actually speak. They very often work with undocumented languages, so they're writing dictionaries and writing grammars. Prescriptive linguistics, and this is probably what you've had the most association with—grammar school teachers, college professors, William Safire's column in the Sunday *New York Times*—prescriptive linguists try and tell us how we should speak, and there's a big distinction here, how we do speak and how we should speak.

It leads to all sorts of political machinations that we probably don't even think about. Dictionaries, for example, who would think that there's a politics of dictionaries? These are just objective documents recording the words in a particular language. But in English dictionaries, there's a wide range of ideological variation. Webster's, for example, is much more willing to accept new words, to include "ain't" or include new technological words, whereas the American Heritage Dictionary is much more conservative, the American Heritage Dictionary leaning toward prescription, Webster's leaning toward description.

The great rule of language is that languages are always changing. In this light, language purity movements are fighting a losing battle. They might slow the pace of change. Take France, for example, very rigid in trying to promote a pure French, it can slow the rate of change, but it can never completely stop it. On the other hand, languages can also be resuscitated from the edge of extinction, and here we can count Welsh, Hebrew. Hebrew was dead for almost 2,000 years, a virtually dead language only spoken by scribes and scholars, and now 3.6 million people speak Hebrew today, the national language of Israel, of course.

We should also keep in mind in making this distinction between prescriptive linguists and descriptive linguists the arbitrariness of grammatical rules. The most famous example, probably, is don't end a sentence with a preposition. This is beaten into us in grammar school and college—don't end a sentence with a preposition—but we can all think of perfectly good sentences that we can end in prepositions. "That's what I was thinking of." "That's where he was going to." In fact, Winston Churchill one time, he spotted a copy editor's remarks in his memoirs where a preposition had been eliminated, and he sent back a missive to this copy editor saying, "This is the sort of English up with which I shall not put." Anthropological linguists work at describing the grammar of languages in a descriptive and not a prescriptive fashion. Prescription often is just an idiosyncrasy that's been codified, that's taken on this status that everybody has to speak in this certain proper fashion, and prepositions at the end of the sentences is one of the best examples.

And linguists, what do linguists do? They describe languages, but also they work in academics and, beyond that, they've long found careers with the CIA, with the military, with the State Department, for example, working as code breakers. A lot of the code breakers of World War II either were linguists or they went on to become linguists, and more recently they branched out into the commercial sector, working for private companies, testing slogans, testing new product names, working with advertising agencies, working as business consultants. The most interesting thing, I think, that linguists have done in recent years, however, concerns the waste isolation pilot project, and this is a project in the U.S. government.

They're creating a place near the Nevada-California border where we can store our highest grade plutonium waste from nuclear weapons production. They want to keep this in a place that's going to be safe for 10,000 years, the half-life of this plutonium, and they're putting it in salt mines, which are very good at soaking up the radioactivity. But they also want signage. They want signs that can be read in 10,000 years warning people of what's there. But what language are we going to speak in 10,000 years? English hasn't been around that long. I mean, just think back to Chaucerian English; we can only understand every other word, words here and there, and that was only 650 years ago. Indo-European, the common language of both Sanskrit and English, is only 4,000 years old. Writing is only 5,000 years old, so how do you create signs that are going to be able to communicate in 10,000 years that there's deadly plutonium at the site?

The linguists working on this commission have developed a couple of different strategies. One is to use pictographs, images, and most famously they used Edvard Munch's *The Scream*, that image, that impassioned, that horrifying image of a person screaming on a bridge, to communicate this idea. They also used a modern-day Rosetta stone, so they include warnings in a variety of languages, including the six official U.N. languages and indigenous languages such as Navajo, with the idea that in 10,000 years in the future, nobody's going to speak English, nobody's going to speak Chinese, nobody's going to speak Russian or German, but by having a warning in all of those different languages they can work out what the warning is. They can break that code.

Finally, let me turn to cultural anthropology. What is culture? Very broadly, culture is everything that people collectively do, think, make, and say. It's an integrated body of beliefs, behavior, technology, ideas shared by a group of people. This is a fine definition, a pretty standard definition, but let me add a couple of important caveats. First of all, culture provides a template for behavior, much more so than strictly prescribing actions. We're not mere cultural automatons, rigidly enacting cultural patterns that have been passed down to us from generations ago. We're creating, we do new things, and it's culture that provides the template for this creation, for this improvisation.

Culture is a way of looking at and acting in the world, and culture significantly overlaps within a given group of individuals, a culture group, but it's also important to keep in mind that culture is never perfectly distributed within a group. We don't all hold to all of the elements of our own culture, but there's enough of significant overlap that allows us to communicate and to create in-group and out-group sorts of allegiances. It's integrated culture; culture is integrated, but it's loosely integrated. Finally, people are generally not aware of their culture; what goes without saying comes without saying. Pierre Bourdieu, a sociologist from France, said that culture is silent about itself as a tradition. It seems normal, our culture seems normal, natural, the only way of doing things. It's what we take for granted.

The study of social anthropology, and this is what is studied in Britain—it's also what the department at Harvard is named—social anthropology implies studying formal legal, economic, and civil structures. Sociology, political science, economics, and social anthropology all work at this level. But culture is more dispositions, it's more ephemeral, it's harder to grasp. It's the presuppositions that we as members of a particular society hold. Of course, the two are intimately connected, but I prefer the moniker "cultural" because it gets at what we have to offer much better.

Like linguists, a number of cultural anthropologists have found employment outside of academia in recent years, particularly in helping large corporations with business consultants and with marketing. General Motors, for example, has employed anthropologists to do shop floor studies, studies of shop floor culture. The United Nations and the World Bank employ anthropologists to help them make their development projects more culturally sensitive. One cultural anthropologist, Clotaire Rapaille, who runs a consultancy called Archetypes International, has helped develop cars—the PT cruiser for Chrysler—and has also advised on advertising for a variety of Ford companies.

One of the most interesting things he did concerns the advertisements, television advertisements of a French importer of French cheeses, importing French cheeses into the United States. And they used as a commercial for their Brie cheese a film, television ad, that had been produced in France and they just used a voice-overlay in English for the States. In the commercial, a woman was picking up unwrapped cheese and squeezing it—you could see her fingerprints on the top of the cheese. She was smelling it, and she was just reveling in this cheesiness of it all, but the television ad wasn't playing in the United States, and they brought in Clotaire Rapaille, this cultural anthropologist, and he said of course it doesn't. The French archetype of cheese is that it's something alive. They relish in the fact that it is living, cultures in cheese. In the United States, our cultural archetype is that cheese is dead, it's sterile. We wrap it tightly in cellophane wrap, and we want to have it not be alive—so some of the interesting things that cultural anthropologists are doing these days.

To conclude, in order to manage the wholism that anthropology strives for, we break down the discipline into these four subfields: biological, archaeological, linguistic, and cultural. At the same time, the greatest strength of the discipline is in bridging these boundaries. For our purposes in this course, physical anthropology can tell us not only about our common evolutionary heritage but about contemporary cultures as well. Take the Maya of Guatemala, with whom I work. It's impossible to understand modern Mayan culture without understanding the civil war that wreaked havoc in Guatemala in the late 1970s and early 1980s, but most of these massacres in Mayan communities were not documented, and the bodies were buried in clandestine graves. Teams of forensic anthropologists are now recording the atrocities of this unwritten history, validating the stories told by survivors.

Likewise, archaeology not only reconstructs the ancient past but also influences the self-perception of groups and even motivates them to redefine their modern cultural forms. Again I mention Arthur Demarest and his work in Conquin in Guatemala in modern Mayan populations. And as we'll explore further in later lectures, linguistics looks not only at abstract language structure but how language is used to form groups and even mold cultural categories. With this background in the four subfields, we move on in the next lectures to discuss concepts of culture in more detail.

Lecture Three
Culture and Relativity

Scope:

The modern anthropological concept of culture has been widely adopted across academic disciplines and in popular discourse. Nineteenth-century anthropologists conceived of culture as singular: Synonymous with civilization, it was seen as something that people possessed to greater and lesser extents. Often, such views were developed as part of evolutionary schemes, the most memorable being Lewis Henry Morgan's "savages, barbarians, and civilization" typology of human societies. By the turn of the 20th century, Franz Boas, a German Jewish immigrant to the United States, was challenging such evolutionary perspectives and developing a pluralistic notion of culture. Boas argued that cultures emerge from historically particular circumstances, not from a universal evolutionary trajectory. Modern definitions stress the malleability and fluidity of culture, although anthropologists have come to see the limits of Boas's cultural relativity.

Outline

I.   The modern discipline of anthropology was born of a 19th-century fascination with science and evolution.

    A. Evolution was very much an idea in the air in 19th-century European intellectual circles.

        1. Charles Darwin gave us the most scientifically plausible mechanism for how evolution works in his theory of natural selection.

        2. The phrase "survival of the fittest" was coined not by Darwin but by Sir Herbert Spencer in a line of thought that has come to be known as "social Darwinism."

    B. Edward B. Tylor (1832–1917) wrote some of the discipline's founding texts and held Oxford University's first position in anthropology (which came to be known as "Mr. Tylor's science").

        1. Tylor gave the most enduring definition of culture: "that complex whole which includes knowledge, belief, art, law, morals, customs and any other capabilities and habits acquired by man as a member of society."

2. Tylor's grand scheme ranked societies along a continuum of progress and unilineal evolution; he was also interested in documenting cultural "survivals," those odd elements left over from times past.

C. In the United States, it was Lewis Henry Morgan (1818–1881) who pioneered anthropology.

1. Morgan, a semi-retired lawyer, became interested in a Seneca group that lived not far from his home in Rochester, New York.

2. After second-hand study of cultures around the world, Morgan devised a scheme of unilineal cultural evolution that progressed from savages to barbarians to civilization.

II. Franz Boas (1858–1942) founded modern American anthropology—earning it academic legitimacy and providing its enduring principle of cultural relativity.

A. Boas's theoretical contributions must be understood in terms of his personal history—as the son of middle-class German Jewish parents and as an immigrant to the United States.

1. Boas pursued studies in geography and physics, writing his Ph.D. dissertation on the "psycho-physics" of the color of sea water.

2. After his compulsory military service, Boas pursued his boyhood dream of making an expedition to the Arctic. There, he lived with the Inuit and was deeply moved by their kindness and humanity; his writings on the Baffin Island people began his career in anthropology.

3. After immigrating to the United States, Boas began to conduct fieldwork among the Kwakiutl people of the northwest coast. He saw this as a form of "salvage ethnography," capturing customs before they died out.

B. Boas fundamentally changed conceptions of "culture."

1. His position must be understood in part as a reaction to the evolutionists.

2. He stressed the historical particularism of each group.

3. He dismantled pseudo-scientific claims about differences between the races.

C. Boas's most enduring contribution has been the perspective of cultural relativity, which holds that observers must suspend their ethnocentrism to understand cultures on their own terms.

   1. The seed of this idea was planted with Boas's study of the color of sea water, in which he noted the culturally relative way the color spectrum is broken up.

   2. This cultural relativity should also apply to values and moral judgments; anthropologists must suspend judgment of other cultures to understand those cultures.

III. Cultural relativity in many ways defines American anthropology and its contribution to society.

   A. The relativistic concept of culture is no longer confined to anthropology—it has been borrowed by other disciplines and entered popular discourse.

   B. As much as we may romanticize cultural relativity and sensitivity, such perspectives are not without their own moral pitfalls.

   1. Boas himself had to rethink cultural relativity in light of the Holocaust.

   2. Where do we draw the line? The case of female circumcision in parts of West Africa offers some suggestions.

Readings:

Franz Boas, *Race, Language, and Culture*.

Ruth Benedict, *Patterns of Culture*.

Clifford Geertz, *The Interpretation of Cultures*.

Questions to Consider:

1. Is it useful to conceive of *culture* in terms of evolution and progress? What does it mean to be a more advanced culture?

2. How has the Boasian perspective influenced definitions of culture?

3. What are the limits of cultural relativity?

Lecture Three—Transcript
Culture and Relativity

I think most anthropologists feel somewhat proprietorial toward the concept of culture, but we also have to take great pride in the fact that it's been widely adopted across academic disciplines and in popular discourse as well. But what is culture exactly? In this lecture, we're going to look at the concept of culture and how it's changed since the 19th century and pioneers such as Edward Tylor and Lewis Henry Morgan. They and other cultural anthropologists considered culture to be singular, synonymous with civilization, and then Franz Boas, the father of American anthropology, turned attention to the multiplicity of cultures and argued for cultural relativity, not judging one's culture's customs by the moral standards of a different culture. The notion of cultural relativity underlies most modern definitions of culture, yet as we'll see in the conclusion to this lecture, cultural relativity has its limits.

As a formal discipline, anthropology only began about 100 years ago, and in the mid-19th century evolution was an idea very much in the air at the time as we mentioned in the last lecture. Darwin and Wallace, Marx, whose scheme was fundamentally evolutionary as well, and less remembered but just as important in his day was Herbert Spencer. Spencer, who was born in 1820 and died in 1903, was an English social philosopher and an early advocate of the theory of evolution. Indeed, he was the one who coined the phrase "survival of the fittest," which is often attributed to Darwin. Spencer's work attempted to combine biology, sociology, ethics, politics, combine all the fields of knowledge into a unified theory organized around the principle of evolution, and this was his basic theory, that things evolve from being less complex to more complex, from being homogenous to being more heterogeneous.

Spencer and his followers attempted to apply natural selection to human societies, and this is a theory that's come to be known as social Darwinism. The social Darwinists argued that human society was like nature in being a competitive arena with limited resources in which individuals fight to survive. Spencer used this to justify laissez-faire capitalism in England and the English class system; he was a staunch Tory. He believed that welfare programs acted against the struggle for survival. They prolonged human suffering by buffering people against the forces of nature. He believed that humans were perfecting themselves and that without government intervention suffering would eventually be eliminated in the world. Certainly our social lives—take workplace politics for example—certainly some aspects of our social lives look like a competitive arena of natural selection, but it's social and not biological, and this is what Spencer crucially missed, was that culture opts us out of evolutionary processes, that culture holds us to a higher moral standard than mere biological imperative.

Like the idea of evolution, the concept of culture was very much in the air in the mid-19th century as well. We could point to a number of scholars who were dancing around the culture concept at the time—Alexander von Humboldt, for example, in Germany—but here we're going to focus on three men who did more than anyone else to establish anthropology as a formal discipline, and they are: Sir Edward B. Tylor, an erstwhile English businessman who became the country's first professor of anthropology; Lewis Henry Morgan, a Rochester, New York, lawyer and parlor intellectual; and finally Franz Boas, a German-Jewish scholar and an emigrant to the United States.

Edward Tylor had become interested in the study of other cultures during a trip to Mexico. He was largely self-taught, but he went on to write the first general textbook in anthropology in 1881, and in 1884 Oxford University created its first readership in anthropology for him, and it was known, the discipline of the time was known as Mr. Tylor's science. He was often called upon in this context to defend the establishment of a whole new discipline. "There are so many subjects to study," people would ask. "why have another academic discipline?" He responded that it's like a backpack. A backpack adds more weight but it allows us to carry everything else. He said that anthropology serves the same function in the academy. It's an additional discipline but brings everything else together and allows us to carry this weight more effectively.

In his book *Primitive Culture*, and this is a title that we would be loath to use these days, but it was published in 1878, he famously defined culture as "that complex whole which includes knowledge, belief, art, law, morals, customs, and any other capabilities and habits acquired by man as a member of society." There are a couple of crucial points here. First of all, Tylor allowed that culture is learned. We're not born with it, it's acquired, and he allowed that culture is shared as a member of society, but let me go back and read the beginning of this quote: "Culture, or civilization, is that complex whole which includes knowledge, belief, art, law morals, customs, and any other capabilities and habits acquired by man as a member of society."

One thing that we see wrong with this definition today is its stress on the singular civilization, or culture, and Tylor believed that all human civilizations followed a single line of evolutionary development, unilineal evolution, and he believed that societies were progressing. Everything was progressing, everything was getting better, but this is unilineal evolution, where everybody is moving in the same direction. All societies are on a scale of evolution, but they're stuck at different levels. Tylor focused on survivals, ancient traits that are still practiced today by primitive peoples due to the weight of tradition, and he focused on survivals because he thought it gave him a window into the past of his own civilization, the past of all of humanity, since he believed that at one time the Europeans were savages as well. In its own way, this is a very progressive sentiment at least for its day. Primitives are real people too; they're just at an earlier stage of cultural development, a cultural infancy or a cultural adolescence, if you will. He believed in the psychic unity of all mankind, that everybody everywhere has the same basic mental capacities, so that he argued that people are all essentially rational and that they learn from their experiences.

Around the time Tylor was writing in England, Lewis Henry Morgan, another armchair anthropologist, as we call them, was pressing forward on the same front in the United States. Morgan was born in 1818 and died in 1881, and he was a wealthy Rochester, New York, lawyer. He had made his money in railroads and then decided to semi-retire and pursue more gentlemanly pursuits. He was a parlor intellectual, and ever since he was a boy he had been fascinated by the Native Americans who lived in New York, and he actually at one point went out and did some fieldwork among the Iroquois and lawyer work as well. He helped the Iroquois fight the U.S. government taking some land away under duress and then he helped to fight this and get their lands back.

While he was working with the Iroquois, he discovered that they viewed their relatives very differently than he did and, being a lawyer, he was sensitive to issues of descent and of kinship and inheritance. The Iroquois are a matrilineal society; they trace descent through female lines. And another interesting thing he found was that they call the children of same-sex siblings by a different name than they call the children of opposite-sex siblings. This is to say that they had two different terms for cousins. They would call one's mother's brother's children cousins, and they would call one's mother's sister's children brother or sister, just as if they were full siblings. He was fascinated by these differences in kinship, he was fascinated by the legal implications, and so he started sending out questionnaires to whites around the world—missionaries, government officials, colonial officials—and asking them about the native peoples, the kinship customs, the technologies and so forth of the native peoples with whom they worked.

He gathered up all of this data, and he published his magnum opus in 1877 called *Ancient Society*. In this, he put forth a model of evolution that had three stages: savagery, barbarism, and civilization, and he believed that all societies progressed through these three stages. Everybody started out as savages, some eventually moved to become barbarians, and, of course, the rest—civilization was Western European civilization and American civilization. There were some key traits that he associated with each of these stages. For example, savages practiced promiscuous sex, barbarians had multiple spouses, multiple wives, and in civilization we had reached the pinnacle of monogamy. Likewise, savages had fire, barbarians had the bow and arrow, and civilization (at the time anyway) had the steam engine, again the pinnacle of technological development.

Like Tylor, Morgan saw societies progressing through a unilinear evolutionary scheme. All groups had or will progress through the stages of savagery, barbarism, and eventually become civilized. While today this perspective seems highly ethnocentric, at the time it was a fairly radical proposition. Savages and barbarians are just as much people as civilized individuals are; they're just at a different stage of development. Morgan was a staunch champion of private property in the state, and these were both hallmarks of Morgan's highest stage of human development, civilization, but Morgan was also truly an evolutionist, and he saw that civilization doesn't mark the end of evolutionary change, and in ancient society, he concluded by noting that "a mere property career is not the final destiny of mankind if progress is to be the law of the future, as it has been of the past."

We have Tylor and we have Morgan, these 19th-century evolutionists, but the edifice built up by these two men was to be torn down by the work of one quite remarkable man, Franz Boas, widely considered to be the father of modern American anthropology. Boas was born in 1858; he died in 1941; he was born in Minden in Germany, Minden, Westphalia, in 1858, two years after Freud was born, interestingly enough. His family was of the prosperous liberal and well-educated German middle class. As a child, he was somewhat sickly. And as is the German custom of that day and even today, his parents would take him to the seashore for cures, and it was during these trips as a young child to the seashore that he decided that one day he would cross the North Sea and go explore the Arctic Circle, a wonderful dream for a small child, but Boas was more intent than most children and their dreams. He would starve himself; he would go on semi-fasts, not eating very much or not eating at all some days to prepare his body for the rigors of such a journey.

In his university studies, and first he studied at Heidelberg and then he went on to Bonn and finally studied at the University of Kiel, Boas applied himself to both geography and physics. In his 1881 doctoral dissertation, it was in physics from the University of Kiel, and it was on the color of seawater. And he initially started out—he was very much concerned with the objective measures of changes in the color of sea water, light intensities, the polarization of light when it's reflected against the water, the absorption of light in the water. But as he was doing this research, he discovered that people perceived these colors differently. Where one person might see green, another might see blue or bluish-green or greenish-blue, and he came to see that there is this subjective quality to perception of colors. This was the kernel of the line of thought that would eventually lead to his definition of culture. Here he's working really at the intersection of hard science and subjective understanding, and it gets us back to what anthropology does best, traveling this divide, trying to be a science, but also trying to offer more humanistic understanding as well.

In 1883, Boas has gone through his state service in Germany, and, fulfilling a childhood dream, he convinces the German Arctic Commission to send him off to the North Pole, or not quite the North Pole but actually to Baffin Island, which is today in the far northwest of Canada, but it's within the Arctic Circle. He was to stay there for a year, and he was going to map Baffin Island and also study the relationship between man and his environment. What better place to study the relationship of man in the environment than such an extreme environmental place. He goes to Baffin Island; he starts living with the Eskimo. Let me mention here that today we call the Eskimo, Inuit. Like the names of many ethnic groups around the world, Eskimo was actually a pejorative. It's a word from a neighboring group, an Algonquin group, and it means dog eater or eater of raw meat. It's not what these people call themselves; they call themselves the Inuit, which means real people.

Anyway, he goes and works among the Inuit, lives and works among the Inuit, and his trip was in many ways a disaster. He arrived late, the winter was exceptionally bad, the hunting was bad, the dogs were dying. He describes these trips where the men would go out and spend 24 to 36 hours wandering around in this really deathly cold. Nonetheless, he was able to survey most of Cumberland Sound and Davis Strait, these sections of Baffin Island, and he did so with the aid of the Inuit. They were able—and he was quite amazed by this— they were able to draw incredibly detailed maps of the coastline, which Boas then used as a basis for drawing his own maps, and he was very much amazed by their sophisticated comprehension of geography.

During his stay, he immersed himself in Inuit culture, living just as they did, and he was very much struck by their basic humanity and generosity. He wrote to his fiancée at the time, "I often ask myself what advantages our good society possesses over those of savages, and I find the more I see of their customs that we have no right to look down upon them. Where among our people could you find such true hospitality?" This experience really sharpened Boas's idea of the basic equality of all peoples, and it wasn't necessarily based on logical reasoning, but on emotion. The kindness and sensitivity these Inuit people had shown him, combined with the behind-the-scenes look that he got of Inuit culture, led him to develop the discipline of anthropology in many ways. "It was with feelings of sorrow and regret," wrote Boas. "that I parted from my Arctic friends. I had seen that they enjoyed life as we do, that nature is also beautiful to them, that feelings of friendship also root in the Eskimo heart, and that the Eskimo was a man just as we are. His feelings, his virtues, and his shortcomings are based on human nature, like ours."

After his work on Baffin Island, Boas returned to Germany, and then fleeing anti- Semitism—of course anti-Semitism was nothing new to Germany; it didn't arise with the Third Reich—he emigrated to the United States, and in the United States he founded anthropology programs at the American Museum of Natural History in New York City and at Columbia University and single-handedly produced a generation of students who went out and founded anthropology programs across the country, establishing the discipline. While in the States, while working at the American Museum of Natural History, he initiated an expedition to the northwest coast of North America to study the northwest coast Indians, and the northwest coast goes from British Columbia up through Alaska.

He worked in particular with a group known as the Kwakiutl. The Kwakiutl are best known for their masks and the totem poles. If you've ever been to the Field Museum in Chicago or the Museum of Natural History in New York City, you can see some of Boas's collections from the Kwakiutl, and he went to the Kwakiutl and he had this notion that he had to do salvage ethnography. The whites are starting to encroach. I have to go in there, Boas thought, and save all of their stories, save all of their legends, record their language, record the grammar and dictionaries, take physical measurements even, and collect all of these artifacts, totem poles and masks and so forth.

This really gets at the heart of Boas's method. Boas stressed that anthropology and our understandings of culture have to be inductive. We don't start out with theory, like Tylor and Morgan had, and then try and prove or disprove it. He says we have to go and live with the people that we're studying, soak all of this information from daily life up and develop theories out of that. Boas argued that cultures are guided by what he called an unreflected logic and that the job of anthropologists is to go in and record this unreflected logic. Boas argued forcefully against the 19th-century evolutionists. He was a German-Jewish immigrant; he had a vested interest in arguing against racial determinism. He argued that humans are born with certain capacities: the capacity to learn a language; the capacity to learn a culture. But what language, what culture, doesn't matter, or rather it's a matter of chance where one is born, the chance circumstances of birth.

One line of thought that Boas is associated with is called today historical particularism, and this was his argument against unilinear evolution. Morgan and Tylor had said that all societies fall along this unilinear chain of development. Boas said no, each culture has its own history, each culture has its own past. Different cultures aren't set upon a unilinear scheme of evolution, but rather there are multiple lines of evolution and development, and to understand the culture we have to look at these bases, their particular circumstances and development.

This came to play most vividly in a dispute he had over mask displays at the American Museum of Natural History, and actually the Smithsonian as well. The normal practice of the day was to group masks together based on how they looked: Let's put all the bird masks in one section; let's put all the fantastical god masks in another section. And Boas said no, based on this principle of historical particularism, we have to put the masks in their cultural context. A mask made by the Kwakiutl is not the same as a bird mask made by the Trobriand Islanders or a bird mask made by the Maya. They all have very different meanings in their own culture, and so he argued that rather than group things together by their aesthetic appearance we have to put them together based on their particular cultural histories. Boas was also an early and an ardent opponent of scientific racism; and think back to the day in the late 19th and early 20th centuries, this was still very much the norm.

In an 1894 address to the American Association for the Advancement of Science, a very controversial speech, he systematically refuted all of the scientific claims for Negro inferiority. Their position in society, he argued, reflects the discrimination against them. Their plight is not the cause of racism— it's the product of racism—and he argues, "We might rather wonder how so much has been accomplished in so short a period of time against such heavy odds." Likewise, he very much argued against discrimination against immigrants, and in 1907 he began a massive study that looked at 18,000 immigrants and their children, immigrants from southern Europe and from eastern Europe, and in measuring their skulls (these were physical anthropology tests), in measuring their skulls, he found that in the first generation the skulls of immigrants approached the size of native-born Americans; and so it wasn't their biology which kept them this way, it was the circumstances in which they lived, their nutrition, and once they were living in an American environment, eating an American diet, their children physically became more like American children.

He used these lines of thought to build up a theory which is known today as cultural relativism. Remember his early work with the color of seawater, that different people perceive of the color of seawater in different ways. Color, as it occurs in nature, the color spectrum of course is a continuum. It documents different wavelength frequencies of light; there are no distinct colors such as green or red given in nature. Our language leads us to break up the spectrum into these neat categories, red, green, blue, and so forth, and languages differ in how they break up the color spectrum. There are some languages in the world that only have two colors, dark and light. Many languages around the world conflate green and blue, a color that linguists often call grue.

He used this idea of people perceiving the world differently to develop the notion of cultural relativity, and this is a central idea in modern cultural anthropology, and it is that a culture has to be evaluated in terms of its own values, not according to the values of another culture, and that these values are relative. One person's terms and categories cannot be transposed to another. There's no culture that's better or worse than another; they're just each products of the unique history. This was very much opposed again to the 19th-century evolutionists, and it was the idea, I think, that most of us probably take for granted these days: Don't judge until you understand the culture. Sometimes this is easy. The Eskimo kiss by rubbing their noses; the Belgians put mayonnaise rather than ketchup on their French fries. Sometimes cultural differences like this, especially the quirky ones, are easy for us to digest.

But very often, the issues are much stickier. My colleague Tom Gregor, for example, works with the Mehinaku in the Amazonian rain forest, and a culturally sanctioned punishment for young girls and for women who have entered into adulterous relationships is gang rape. And one time he reports that he was in the field and a young woman was accused of having sex with another young man, and the men in the village were preparing to rape this woman. In circumstances like this, and fortunately in that circumstance, the tensions diffused and nothing happened, but he had to make this choice. This is the tradition of another culture. I'm a cultural anthropologist, I need to be sensitive to this, but where do we draw that line? Where is it OK to step in and say, "No, that's over the boundary, and we have to take action"?

We could take Nazi Germany as well, and this is where Boas really had to modify his own views of cultural relativity. An extreme cultural relativistic point of view would say "Nazi Germany, the ideology of National Socialism, this is the product of German culture; we have to take it as that. We can't judge it based on our own sentiments." But of course we do judge such things, and Boas himself backed off from his extreme cultural relivism in the early days of World War II. But in a broader, more practical sense, cultural relativity means temporarily suspending judgment of other people's customs and practices until we can understand those customs and practices on their own terms. The debate these days about cultural relativity, one debate these days, focuses on the practice of female circumcision, and this is the removal of the clitoris, surgical removal of the clitoris.

Female circumcision was practiced in the United States and Europe through the 1800s as a medical treatment for masturbation, and it's still practiced today in large parts of Africa, particularly Muslim areas of Africa. In Somalia, for example, girls are circumcised when they're between the ages of six and 12, somewhere in there. The operation is performed without anesthetics in not sterile conditions. The girl is normally restrained by an older woman, circumcised with a razor blade, but after this the girl is no longer a girl, she's a woman, and the staunchest advocates for this, even in Somalian society, are the women themselves, arguing that women have to go through this process to not be girls anymore but to become true women, and it also offers the additional benefit of being able to visually prove virginity at the time of a wedding. Most Westerners find this custom of female circumcision repulsive, and the World Health Organization has even condemned female genital mutilation, but it continues to be widely practiced, and again it's even advocated by the women themselves. Not all Somalian women are proponents of female circumcision, but a fair number are, and this is one of those ironic circumstances where human rights is at odds with cultural diversity.

We've come a long way in terms of our understanding of culture from the work of Spencer and Tylor and Morgan and their evolutionary scheme of things. Boas's concept of cultural relativity is widely held not only in the academy but throughout society. We often speak of multiculturalism, cultural sensitivity, and so on. This is part of our vocabulary today, and yet now more than ever we're faced with the difficult moral questions and this question of the limits of cultural relativity. Where do we draw the line? At what point must ethical obligations trump respect for cultural differences and force us to take action? We could all probably agree that genocide is beyond the pale, but what about female circumcision? Is a woman's right to have her body intact more important than the right to respect the traditions of other cultures? What about when women's rights come into conflict with cultural rights? These are issues that we're having to grapple with these days.

In the next lecture, we'll look at the work of two cultural anthropologists who have really pressed the envelope in this issue of cultural relativity and strongly advocated for an extreme position of cultural relativity and changed the discipline of anthropology in doing so.

Lecture Four
Fieldwork and the Anthropological Method

Scope:

Anthropologists are drawn to the exotic otherness of distant locales, and no other place has held more romantic fascination for Western observers than the Pacific Islands. Two early anthropological pioneers, Bronislaw Malinowski and Margaret Mead, are particularly associated with Pacific studies. In 1915, Malinowski traveled to the Trobriand Islands off the coast of northern New Guinea, where he would live for two years. Documenting the Trobrianders' matrilineal kinship system, Malinowski challenged the universality of Freud's Oedipal theories, showing that tensions between father and son were nonexistent in Trobriand society. Margaret Mead, a student of Franz Boas, traveled to Samoa at the tender age of 23, to prove theories of cultural relativity. Like Malinowski, she found a much more sexually liberated culture with fewer conflicts between adolescents and their parents than was the case in the West. Mead's data have since been challenged, but recent research on the meaning of sex on Samoa partially vindicates her view.

Outline

I. Cultural anthropology's primary methodological tool is participant observation—actually going and living with the people being studied to gain a more intimate understanding of their daily lives.

    A. Extended fieldwork is a hallmark of modern cultural anthropology.

    B. The process is often referred to as "doing ethnography," which is documenting the lifeways of another culture in a sensitive fashion. Doing ethnography primarily involves participant observation and other forms of social science data collection.

    C. Cultural anthropologists write their results in *ethnographies*, representations of other cultures.

II. The greatest early champion of anthropological fieldwork was Bronislaw Malinowski (1884–1942).

    A. Born in what is today Poland, Malinowski studied at the University of Cracow, where he received his Ph.D. with the highest honors of the Austrian Empire.

        1. Malinowski went on to study in Germany and, finally, at the London School of Economics in its burgeoning anthropology department.

        2. At the outbreak of World War I in 1914, Malinowski was on his way to study a small group off the coast of New Guinea. As an enemy national in allied territory (via Australia), Malinowski was not allowed to travel back to Europe.

        3. Making a virtue of this necessity, Malinowski became the biggest proponent of conducting long-term fieldwork and participant observation.

    B. Malinowski ended up spending two years living among the Trobriand Islands off the east coast of New Guinea.

        1. Malinowski was struck by the matrilineal kinship system of the Trobrianders and the jockeying among chiefs for power.

        2. Malinowski was a prolific writer, and his oeuvre covers everything from marriage and sexuality to trade and subsistence goods.

        3. Malinowski shows why Trobrianders use magic in building long-distance canoes—to symbolically tame forces outside of their control—but not in building other sorts of canoes.

    C. Malinowski's view of culture was, like Boas's, fundamentally relativistic.

        1. He viewed cultures as integrated wholes, the parts of which all served a particular function.

        2. He disproved that native peoples were somehow irrational, showing that within their cultural contexts, natives act perfectly rationally.

        3. He argued against the universalizing of Freudian theories of the Oedipus complex, showing that the tensions between father and son did not hold true in the Trobriands.

III. Margaret Mead (1901–1978), a student of Franz Boas, conducted fieldwork in the Pacific islands not long after Malinowski. She went on to become the public face of anthropology in the last half of the century.

    A. A student of Franz Boas, Mead was driven by Boasian ideals.

        1. Like Boas, she saw the field as a laboratory to test social theories.

        2. Like Malinowski, she sought to disprove universal psychological theories. In their place, she proposed a Boasian relativity.

    B. In 1925, at age 23, Mead headed off to do fieldwork in Samoa. Her work would later be published in the best-selling *Coming of Age in Samoa*.

        1. Mead was attracted to the romantic view of Polynesia in the popular imagination.

        2. She spent a lot of time with adolescent girls and young women.

        3. She wrote about Samoans' adolescent sexual freedom.

        4. She used these data to argue against the Freudian notion of a conflict-ridden adolescence and contrasted the Samoans positively with contemporary U.S. culture.

    C. Mead's data were later attacked by Derek Freeman, an anthropologist who studied in Samoa in the 1940s.

IV. Modern definitions of culture tend to stress its dynamic, ever-changing nature.

    A. We generally conceive of culture as learned and shared, but it is shared to varying degrees.

    B. Culture is not so much a "thing" as a process, a text being written.

    C. Clifford Geertz sees culture as a text to be interpreted; Michael Herzfeld views cultural anthropology as the study of "common sense."

Readings:

Bronislaw Malinowski, *Argonauts of the Western Pacific*.

Margaret Mead, *Coming of Age in Samoa*.

Michael Young, *Malinowski's Kiriwina.*

Questions to Consider:

1. What sorts of data can participant observation yield that other methodologies miss?

2. Why might the Pacific Islands hold such a fascination for Victorian-era Europeans?

3. Do Margaret Mead's critics negate her social observations, or do they still hold true?

Lecture Four—Transcript
Fieldwork and the Anthropological Method

We anthropologists distinguish ourselves from most of the other social sciences based on our emphasis on fieldwork: going there, wherever there may be, to study them, whoever they may be. We build our theoretical models not out of ivory tower ruminations but from observed experience. As an anthropologist, I'm very much concerned with observable behavior, what people do rather than what they should do. Political scientists and sociologists and economists develop abstract models of human behavior, very interesting abstract models that tell us a lot about human behavior, but anthropology has a lot to offer in building up theory from fieldwork, from data that we gather on the ground. In the lecture today, we focus on the ethnographic fieldwork of two anthropological pioneers, Bronislaw Malinowski and Margaret Mead, both of whom were drawn to life in the Pacific. Malinowski worked in the Trobriand Islands, Mead worked in Samoa, and their writing set the early standard for 20th-century ethnographic fieldwork.

What is ethnography? Cultural anthropologists do ethnography. The term comes to us from the Greek *ethnos*, which means race or people or ethnicity, and *graph*, writing or representation of. Thus, ethnography is writing about other peoples, but ethnography, the way in which cultural anthropologists use it, refers to both a process, doing ethnography, and a product, the ethnography, a book that we wind up with. In terms of the process, it involves participant observation, going and living in the place being studied for an extended period of time, and learning the culture as a child, learning the culture from the inside out. We gather data; we have a number of methods for data gathering. We do formal and informal interviews, we map out fields, we conduct surveys, we do time allocation studies, we look at the caloric intake of families, and so forth, but we also try and get a more subjective understanding, walking in the shoes of the people who we're studying. That's the process of doing ethnography.

The act of writing ethnography, we come back, digest all of this information that we've gathered and write it up, using the minutiae of everyday life that we've gathered in the field to interrogate larger issues, theories, stereotypes, public policy even, whatever it may be. In this, as Boas pointed out, anthropology is fundamentally inductive rather than eductive, building up theory from all of this data that we find in the field. Morgan did some fieldwork with the Iroquois, as we have mentioned. Boas saw the importance of fieldwork and instilled this in his students, but it was Bronislaw Malinowski who became the most vocal proponent of long-term modern fieldwork.

Malinowski was born in 1884; he died in 1942; he was born in Krakow, what is today Poland but at the time was part of the Austrian empire; his parents were minor Polish nobility, his father an expert in Polish folk dialects. At school, Malinowski studied physics and math with an additional emphasis on philosophy, and note here that, like Boas, there's a blurring of the boundary between what were considered to be hard sciences and the softer humanities. He received his Ph.D. in 1908; dissertation was on the principle of economic thought, and it was conferred with the highest honors of the Austrian empire, *Sub auspiciis Imperatoris*. He went on to Leipzig to study folk psychology and continued moving westward and moving toward the discipline of anthropology, eventually winding up in London, studying under an early anthropologist, Edward Westermark, in this burgeoning new field at the London School of Economics.

In 1914, he got a fellowship to go and study the peoples of an island Malus, off the coast of New Guinea, and when he was traveling there, he was traveling, first to Australia, and this was going to be his home base during his fieldwork, but as he was traveling en route, World War I broke out. This is in 1914, World War I, 1914-1918, and he found himself an enemy alien in Allied territory. He had been born in Krakow, he was an Austrian citizen, and so the Australian authorities were very kind, given the circumstances, once he reached there. They allowed him to travel around Australia, travel around in New Guinea, which was part of Australia, even helped fund some of his exploration and research, but they wouldn't allow him to go back home, wouldn't allow him to go back to Europe. He was stuck, and what was meant to be a relatively brief trip turned into a several years' stay.

His fieldwork, he began by exploring some of the islands off the coast of what is today Papua New Guinea, and you'll remember that New Guinea is divided into two parts today. The western part is part of Indonesia; the eastern part is Papua New Guinea. And in 1915 he goes to the Trobriand Islands, which are located off the coast of New Guinea, off the southeast coast of New Guinea. He stayed there for a year, from 1915 to 1916. He returned briefly to Australia for a respite, and then went back to the Trobriand Islands from 1917 to 1918. Thus he spent two years in total on the Trobriand Islands, and he became the most vocal proponent of what would become anthropology's signature method, participant observation, but really he was making a virtue out of a necessity. He couldn't go back to England even if he wanted to; he couldn't go back to Krakow even if he wanted to. He had to stay in the Trobriand Islands, but having been forced to do that, he saw the value in long-term fieldwork, long-term participant observation, and he compelled the discipline out of its armchair.

He learned the local language, he lived in the local communities, and he generally took part in everyday life. Allow me to read a quote from one of his books where he describes his early fieldwork experience: "Imagine yourself suddenly set down, surrounded by all your gear, alone on a tropical beach, close to a native village, while the launcher dinghy which had brought you sails away out of sight. Since you take up your abode in the compound of some neighboring white man, trader, or missionary, you have nothing to do but to start at once on your ethnographic work. Imagine further that you're a beginner without previous experience, with nothing to guide you and no one to help you, for the white man is temporarily absent or else unable to waste any of his time. This exactly describes my first initiation into fieldwork on the south coast of New Guinea. I well remember the long visits I paid to the villages in those first weeks, the feelings of hopelessness and despair after many obstinate but futile attempts had entirely failed to bring me into real touch with the natives or supply me with any material. I had periods of despondency, when I buried myself in the reading of novels, as a man might take to drink in a fit of tropical depression and boredom."

The culture he found in the Trobriands, he was eventually able to break into Trobriand society and to commune with the Trobrianders as much as he could, and the culture that he found there was radically different than anything he'd ever encountered. The Trobriand Islands are a group; there are four main islands, numerous small ones off the coast of New Guinea. The main island where

Malinowski worked is called Kiriwina. The Trobrianders are a matrilineal society. Descent and kinship are traced through women, not men, and you'll recall that it was the matrilineality of the Iroquois that had piqued Lewis Henry Morgan's interest in anthropology as well. The Trobrianders were also a classic chiefdom, a ranked chiefdom. Certain families were ranked higher than others; there were chiefly families, there were noble families, and there were commoners, and there were various levels of chiefs as well.

He found a society that was in some ways infatuated with the yam. Yams were the staple crop of Trobriand society, but they were also the symbolic part of Trobriand society. Yams formed much of the wealth of Trobriand males. He found a system where there were intricate trade networks connecting these islands with one another and trade not only in subsistence goods but in symbolic items as well. We're going to have a chance to come back to Trobriand culture later in this course, and it's a fascinating place and Malinowski was very much taken by it, and living there for as long as he did allowed him to go beyond just the most striking exotic customs, just the most unusual things, to look at what he called the imponderabilia of everyday life.

Malinowski wrote widely on a wide variety of topics. He wrote about Trobriand gardening, he wrote about Trobriand magic, he wrote about trade, he wrote about sex, and he did more than almost anyone else to popularize anthropology, especially in England. To give you an idea, these are some of the titles of his books published in the 1920s and '30s: *Crime and Custom in a Savage Society*; *Myth in Primitive Psychology*; *The Sexual Life of Savages*; *Coral Gardens and their Magic*, wonderful titles, wonderful catchy titles, but also all very fine-grained ethnographic analyses, the sort of work that we still read today in anthropology because of its vivid and comprehensive descriptions of Trobriand life.

I will mention here in passing that his diary was published posthumously. Now his daughter, in fact, wrote the preface and edited parts of the diary, and it turns out, based on this, and it was supposed to be a very private diary, but it turns out that he was also bad-tempered, he was contemptuous of the natives at times, he was a bit of a misogynist, he had very explicit sexual fantasies, but, as the quote I read a moment ago said, he was on the verge of going crazy at times, literally isolated, the only person who spoke his own language, no one much to interact with. And in his vindication, I should note that he always publicly argued very vigorously against racial prejudices, and, in fact, one of his students—after he got back to England, he started teaching at the London School of Economics—and one of his students was Kenyata, the future independence leader of Kenya, and many of his students stressed how much he valued cultural diversity and fought against entrenched racial prejudices of the time. So, like Boas, Malinowski came to the conclusion that societies or cultures are integrated and that one must study them as integrated wholes.

Also, like Boas, Malinowski stressed the native perspective on things, an emic perspective, a perspective from inside the culture, and he was very much concerned with cultural context. He said that if somebody understands why a native person, a Trobriander, does a certain custom that we might find odd, if you understand it within the cultural context, there's a logic to what they're doing. We might not understand that logic, but they do, and they're just as logical, just as reasonable as ourselves, but they have a different set of resources and knowledge to work with. Malinowski showed that there was always a logic if we understood the full cultural context. He's reported to have once run into a cannibal in New Guinea and it's said that the cannibal asked him, "What were the Europeans doing with all of these bodies that were being killed during World War I? How did the Europeans eat all of that flesh?" Malinowski said, "You know, well, we don't eat the bodies," and the cannibal replied, "That's crazy, that's barbaric. Why would you kill without any real object?" So, like Boas, Malinowski was very much concerned with cultural relativity

He also, in terms of theory, he promoted a theory called, which we call today anyway, functionalism, and this is the idea that every custom in a society serves some sort of function, and we could divide these up into three main types. There are basic functions, shelter, food, sex, and so forth. There are integrated functions, customs that keep the society integrated as a whole. And there are psychological functions, and a couple of examples of the psychological functions: He noted, for example, that the Trobrianders are very proficient gardeners. They can grow these huge yams, and yet they religiously follow certain rites, certain magical rites, when they're doing their planting. He said, "Why would they do that? They're such wonderful gardeners. Why do they have to resort to magic in their gardening?" He concluded that it was because they were trying to control those variables outside of their control, the weather, things that they could not possibly control; they took recourse to magic to try and bring those into their own control.

The same thing holds true for canoes. He noted that the canoes that the Trobriand islanders built for traveling in the inlets and bays around the islands, they were nothing special, that people would just build them and there were no special rites or rituals that went along with it. But for their long-distance voyaging commutes, there was an elaborate ritual process that had to go into building the canoes, and the reason why, Malinowski argued, was to relieve their anxiety over these uncertain conditions of weather and the sea that they had no control over at all. So he said that lots of magical customs, they serve to relieve people's anxieties about the future, to, in his words, "to ritualize man's optimism." Likewise with the family, he said that the family served a function in society, and that function was to satisfy certain basic human needs, to domesticate sex, to cope with caring for a child and training a child, and to serve as the locus for the primary emotional attachments and social ties of individuals. Malinowski's contribution was, much like Boas's, stressing cultural relativity in the study of other cultures. The natives, they're not primitives, they're not savages, they just have a different set of values and perhaps a different logical structure than we do.

So as Malinowski was shaking things up in England in the 1920s with these racy titles of his books, Margaret Mead, who was a student of Boas's, was doing the same thing in the United States. Mead was younger than Malinowski; she was also more self-consciously provocative than Malinowski, and she was getting Americans to think about their own and other cultures in new ways. Mead was born in 1901; she died in 1978, a proper middle-class Midwestern Episcopalian girl. In 1920, she goes to New York City, she transfers to Barnard College, which is associated with Columbia University, and she starts hanging out in the wonderfully vibrant counterculture of New York City in the 1920s, in Greenwich Village, the questioning of gender roles, the fight for women's rights, the questioning of sexual norms and so forth, and in her senior year in college she takes a class from Franz Boas, and she's hooked. She says, "This is what I have to do. Anthropology is what I've been looking for."

She goes on and she writes her M.A. thesis under Boas, looking at the correlation of IQ tests, or looking at IQ test results of immigrant children, particularly Italian immigrants in the States, and this was building on Boas's earlier work where he had looked at head size, skull shapes and sizes of immigrant children, and what Mead found was that there was a close correlation of the native language of the household and how well children did on IQ tests. At the time, a number of people were arguing that the immigrants are getting stupider every year as they come over, and we're doing these IQ tests as they get off the boat to show that they're getting dumber. What Mead showed was that wasn't the case at all. The better someone spoke English, the better they did on an IQ test, and so the longer children of immigrants had been in the States, the better they did on these IQ tests. They weren't naturally mentally inferior, just different, something we would take for granted today, but at the time, in the 1920s, it was rather revolutionary.

In 1925, she sets off for Samoa. She wants to go and do fieldwork in this most exotic of locations, Samoa. She's 23 years old, she's five feet, two and a half inches tall, 98 pounds., and this really gutsy young woman—and this was no small journey in those days. A train trip across the country, she stopped in Santa Fe and dropped off a friend, went to the west coast, got on a ship and set sail for Pago Pago, and this was where she was going to do her work—it was the capital of American Samoa at the time—but once she gets there, she decides it's been too corrupted by American missionaries and American colonial officials, and so she changes course for the island of Tau, and she goes there because "It was the most primitive and unspoiled area of Samoa." There was this pull; I've got to go to the place that's been least corrupted by Western civilization to record their culture for future generations.

She saw the field as a laboratory to test various hypotheses, and primarily she went into the field to test the hypothesis that a troubled adolescence was universal and necessary, and this is something that Freud at least implied, and a number of Freudians were expanding, that adolescent conflict between children and their parents is inherent the world over. But Mead sets out to prove Boasian cultural relativity, and this is something that went very well with her gender politics as well. She was fighting for women's rights, and she saw that these were cultural constructions, the way in which women and men were conceived, and she believed that this was also the case of children and parents. She was conducting a type of salvage ethnography; she wanted to go in and save these customs before they died away, before the decline brought about by the influence of whites and missionaries and colonists.

Working on Samoa, she learned the language. We're not sure how well, but she learned the language and she worked mostly with adolescent girls, 60 girls in particular. She got most of her information from 25 girls, and these were teenagers and early twenties, and most of her data came from just two individuals, two key informants, and she strived for a subjective understanding of what life was like on Samoa. She recorded lots of gossip, lots of stories and so forth, and she came back and she wrote a book in 1928 called *Coming of Age in Samoa*, which became a nationwide bestseller. In this book, what she described was that adolescence in Samoa was largely smooth. It was free of the conflict that we find in American society, and she tied this to the freer norms of sexuality on Samoa.

She said that young children, girls and boys, are encouraged to experiment sexually. Very often, older men will initiate younger women into the pleasures of sex. She writes of the adolescents going off and romping, having sex underneath the palm trees, the custom of young adolescent boys sneaking out of their houses at night, after everyone has fallen asleep, and sneaking into their lovers' house and sleeping with their lover and then waking up before anyone else the next morning and leaving. She writes that sex was the pastime par excellence for the Samoans.

She admitted that there were differences. Samoan society was a chiefdom, like the Trobriand Islanders. There were different rankings of families, and the chiefly families had certain obligations, and, among these, chiefly families would choose one of their daughters to become a ceremonial virgin. It was called a *taupu*, and these girls were expected to maintain their virginity until there was a defloration ceremony at marriage, and it brought a lot of honor on the chiefs' families to have a taupu in the house. But, given this exception among chiefly families, she said that with this major intergenerational conflict, control over sexuality, parents trying to control the children's sexuality, that there were really no adolescent tensions on Samoa.

She writes, "Growing up can be free, easy, and uncomplicated. Romantic love as it occurs in our civilization, inflexibly bound up with our ideas of monogamy, exclusiveness, jealousy, and undeviating fidelity, does not occur in Samoa." This was proof of Papa Franz, as she called Boas, of Papa Franz's theories of relativity over these Freudian notions of the universal elements of human culture. After the publication of *Coming of Age in Samoa* in 1928, she becomes really a national star up until her death in 1978, playing to a growing liberal sensibility in the United States, a growing interest and willingness to talk about sex. She had a column in *Redbook*, she was on the *Merv Griffin Show*, she was the public face of anthropology for at least a generation, if not a couple of generations.

Another anthropologist, Derek Freeman, had worked in Samoa after Mead; he worked there in the '40s, so some 20 years later, and after Mead's death, in 1983, Freeman published a book which debunked a lot of what Mead had argued for Samoa. He says that in fact virginity was highly valued among Samoans; yes, by the elites, yes, by the chiefs, but that this had trickled down to the commoners as well. He notes that Samoa has a relatively low rate of pregnancy. If everybody's going off and having sex underneath the palms, why isn't there a higher pregnancy rate? He says that Mead romantically confused rape with consensual sex, that these night crawlers, these young adolescents who had left their homes to crawl into the homes of their girlfriends, this wasn't romantic lovers meeting illicitly, this was rape, and he argues that the girls of Samoa intentionally tricked Mead, that there is a cultural valuation of teasing other people and tricking other people, and that her informants played to what she was wanting to hear and told her these fantastic stories about their sex lives.

Whatever the case, and there's been a wealth of data produced over the last years supporting Mead and attracting for Mead, and we're not really sure what went on, but Mead's notions of cultural relativity and bringing it to the fore of U.S. society and really putting it in people's faces shook up American popular culture and our notions of what is acceptable, and of cultural relativity. And this relativity, put forth by Boas, put forth by Malinowski, put forth by Mead, underwrites our modern understanding of culture, not only in anthropology but in popular culture as well and popular usage as well.

Let me add a couple of things to this cultural relativity. First of all, that culture is dynamic; it's a constantly changing process, a creative dynamic process. It's like a text being written, like jazz or improvisation. We play off of themes, we develop our own riffs, and in this light it's interesting to listen to a quote by Clifford Geertz in his book *The Interpretation of Cultures*: "The culture of a people is an ensemble of texts, themselves ensembles, which the anthropologist strains to read over the shoulders to whom they properly belong." I love this image of the anthropologist straining to read over the shoulder of an informant, this text of culture that's constantly being written. Culture's not a thing; it's not a list of traits but an ongoing creation. Just as we ourselves are not cultural automatons, acting out preordained roles, neither are the Sherpa, neither are the Bedouins, neither are the Trobrianders, neither are the Samoans.

A lot of times we give ourselves more cultural leeway they we do these other ethnic groups. Of course we're creative, of course our culture is constantly being changed, but we tend to view other ethnic groups as being more static in some way. Michael Herzfeld defines anthropology as the study, the comparative study of common sense, the things we take for granted, just the way the world is, and that's what we do as anthropologists in many ways. We study other common senses; we juxtapose those with our own way of doing things to shake up our conceptions of the world, and this is what Malinowski and Mead did so well. Geertz, going back to Clifford Geertz, his book, *The Interpretation of Cultures*, Geertz also defines ethnography for us, and let me read this "Doing ethnography is establishing rapport, selecting informants, transcribing text, taking genealogies, mapping fields, keeping a diary and so on, but it's not these things, techniques or received procedures, that define the enterprise. What defines it is the type of intellectual effort it is, an elaborate venture in thick description." Thick description, thick description in Geertz's words, is looking for the multiplicity of possible meanings in any given situation.

The example he uses is, let's say a person closes one eye and opens it again rapidly. What goes on there? It could be a twitch; the person might have a neurological disorder that makes him twitch. Perhaps it's a wink. Is their information trying to be communicated? Maybe it's somebody parodying another person who has a twitch, so maybe it's someone parodying another person's winks, so there can be multiple winks upon winks upon winks, if you will, and this is the problem of anthropology, and what anthropologists strive to do is to uncover these complexities, to divine the difference between a wink and a twitch or a sincere wink communicating information or a parody wink.

Whatever the faults of fieldwork, and Malinowski's legacy is tainted by his diary, as we'll see later in the course, it seems like he missed a number of female aspects to Trobriand society. Mead's study has been contested by Freeman and others, but, whatever the faults of their fieldwork, we still read both Malinowski and Mead today for their evocative and deep descriptions of native life in the Trobriand Islands and on Samoa.

Lecture Five
Nature, Nurture, and Human Behavior

Scope:

Questions of nature versus nurture have intrigued thinkers throughout the ages. How much of who we are is determined by biology, and how much is learned culture? The relatively recent field of sociobiology (or evolutionary psychology) addresses these questions by looking for evolutionary origins for social behavior. Biologists have traditionally defined evolutionary "fitness" in terms of individuals—how long they live and how many offspring they produce. Sociobiologists shift the focus from individuals to genes. Stemming from studies of ants, bees, and other social insects, sociobiology sees individuals as simply containers for genes. This, in turn, allows them to show an evolutionary basis for altruism and nepotism.

Sociologists also study "attractiveness" from an evolutionary perspective. They argue that evolutionary pressures act differently on men than on women, producing different conceptions of what is considered attractive (most simply, that men value physical beauty and youthful appearance while women are more concerned with character and social status). Recent cross-cultural studies of conceptions of beauty, however, call into question the universality of sociological claims.

Outline

I. To what extent is human behavior determined by nature and to what extent through nurture? This question has long plagued philosophers and social thinkers, and it gets to the heart of anthropology.

   A. John Locke famously weighed in on the side of nurture with his *tabula rasa* idea of human development. Most cultural anthropologists today emphasize cultural development over biological determinism.

   B. The case for biological determinism in human nature has a dubious past, associated with eugenics and racism. Shedding this taint, the field of sociobiology (or evolutionary psychology) has emerged to uncover genetic bases for human behavior.

II. Sociobiology builds on Darwin's theory of natural selection and advances in our understanding of genetics to redefine what is meant by evolutionary "fitness."

  A. The synthetic approach to evolution combined Darwinian selection with Mendelian genetics and the discovery of DNA's structure.

  B. Sociobiology emerged in the mid-1970s, offering a new synthesis.
    1. E. O. Wilson, on the basis of his work with social insects, put forth a comprehensive theory of the evolutionary bases of cooperation.
    2. Richard Dawkins captured the core idea of sociobiology with his phrase "the selfish gene."
    3. Sociobiologists point out that *Homo sapiens* evolved in a particular environment (the environment of evolutionary adaptation, or EEA), roughly corresponding to the Pleistocene period from 1.8 million to about 11,000 years ago. Early in the development of *Homo sapiens*, culture came to trump environmental pressures on evolution. Thus, our basic biological adaptation is to a Pleistocene environment.

  C. Sociobiologists base much of their theory on a reconceptualization of "fitness."
    1. Fitness is generally considered to be an individual's direct success in reproducing.
    2. Sociologists argue that we should look at humans as containers of genes—it is not so important if the individual survives or dies or reproduces, but how many of his or her genes get passed down to the next generation.
    3. As genes are shared among related individuals, sociologists argue for the concept of "inclusive fitness," which takes into account the survival not only of individuals but of the genes they carry.
    4. Thus, it sometimes makes evolutionary sense for individuals to sacrifice themselves for their relatives.

III. Sociobiologists have contributed to our understanding of altruism and reciprocity, reproductive strategies between the sexes, and the biological basis of attractiveness.

    A. Dawkins's selfish genes ironically result in sociability. Altruism and reciprocity—the glue of social relations—actually provide a selective advantage to the genes of a person.

    B. Sociobiologists have posited fundamentally different pressures at work on men and women in their reproductive strategies.

        1. Humans pursue what is termed a *K strategy* of reproduction—having very few offspring but investing greatly in their care. This is made necessary by the long period of helplessness that characterizes human offspring.

        2. Using an economic metaphor, sociologists argue that sperm is in plentiful supply while eggs are in short supply. This results in men and women having different goals and strategies.

        3. This line of thought argues that men are looking for youth, fidelity, and health in women, while women look for material success and commitment in men.

    C. Sociobiologists also study the biology of sexual attractiveness.

        1. They argue that men prefer younger women to maximize childbearing potential, as well as a certain waist-to-hip ration that indicates childbearing potential.

        2. Nonetheless, a number of these traits seem to be specific to U.S. culture, calling into question the universal applicability of the theory.

Readings:

Richard Dawkins, *The Selfish Gene*.

E. O. Wilson, *On Human Nature*.

Desmond Morris, *The Naked Ape*.

Robin Wright, *The Moral Animal*.

Questions to Consider:

1. To what extent is our behavior predetermined by our genes?

2. Do men and women have fundamentally different goals for marriage and mating?

3. Can "subjective" attractiveness be based in genetic predispositions?

Lecture Five—Transcript
Nature, Nurture, and Human Behavior

In this lecture, we turn to the eternal question of nature versus nurture. Now this is a phrasing that comes to us from Prospero's description of Caliban in *The Tempest*, which says, "A devil, a devil born, on whose nature nurture can never stick." So what part of who we are as individuals is determined by birth and how do such innate predispositions affect culture? Mainstream anthropology comes down firmly on the nurture side of this debate. Since the times of Boas, we've argued against scientific racism; we've argued that culture can be determinate in who we grow up to be.

At the same time, we must acknowledge that we're biological beings, that we live within the bodies that were given, although perhaps less so in these days of plastic surgery, and there's certainly give and take between biology and cultural constraints and possibilities, and it's at this nexus between biology and culture that sociobiologists, also called evolutionary psychologists, look for common elements, common elements across cultures and trying to look back and see which of these common elements might have a genetic basis, might have some sort of evolutionary cause. In this lecture we're going to look at what sociobiologists have to tell us about altruism and nepotism, attractiveness and mating strategies. The question is how much of who we are is determined at birth. In contemporary terms, this would mean how much of who we are is genetically given, and these questions really hit at the heart of anthropology.

On the one hand, we as anthropologists argue that all humans are fundamentally alike, at least biologically. We're all Homo sapiens, we're all members of the same species, and further subspecies differentiation is virtually meaningless at the genetic level, and yet, in addition to setting the commonalities of humans, this fundamental similarity of humans, we anthropologists also study the many differences between human populations, what makes us different, the different marriage patterns, different kinship patterns, different sorts of religious beliefs, political organization, and so forth, so this idea of what is natural and what is given to us by culture gets at the heart of anthropology. For predecessors to this, we can look back to Herbert Spencer and the social Darwinists of the 19th century, who argued that who we are is determined at birth. We could look at John

Locke and his idea of the *tabula rasa*, that children are born a blank slate on which everything that we learn in life is written after we're born. Who we become as adults is based on what we learn as children.

Before we get deeper into a discussion of sociobiology, I want to talk a little bit about the politics of this discipline, or the sub-discipline. Actually, there are sociobiologists who are anthropologists, there are sociobiologists who are psychologists, there are sociobiologists who are biologists as well, and a number of them these days prefer the term evolutionary psychologist to distance themselves from the negative implications that sociobiology has taken on over the years. Now I think that there is a resistance to sociobiological explanations, in part because we like to see ourselves as unique, as humans. We don't like to see ourselves as animals; we like to see ourselves set apart, and so looking for biological explanations for our behavior offends our sensibilities in some way. But it's also a fact that looking for any sort of explanation for human behavior is tainted by histories of racism, the histories of eugenics, the Nazi ideologies of trying to create a superhuman race, these Ubermensch, by breeding what they thought were particularly good-looking human beings, so looking at the biological bases of behavior has this taint of eugenics as well.

There's also the taint of racism in looking for biological bases for behavior. Take IQ tests, for example; there are vast differences in cultural responses to IQ tests, and we've found that IQ tests are extremely culturally dependent. If you were brought up in a Western culture, which values this linear logical way of thinking, you'd probably do quite well on standardized tests such as the IQ test. People from other cultures around the world, who don't share our same linearity of logic, do very poorly on IQ tests, and this doesn't mean that they're stupid, it doesn't mean they don't have the same sort of mental capacities that we have, they just see the world in a different way, and thus it's a way that's not measured very well by IQ tests. We can look at correlations between IQ and race and a number of books in recent years have done this, *The Bell Curve* most famously, but what does this really tell us?

It really tells us more about the different cultures of the people rather than biological differences between them, rather than differences in what their minds can think. And it's telling us more—at least in the

United States, where most of these studies have been done—about economic status. It turns out that economic status is a much better indicator of IQ test results than is race. It just so happens that in the U.S. race is highly correlated with economic status, and so it's easy to confuse these variables in the cause and effect here. This is just to give you an idea of some of the reasons why sociobiology has been viewed by some as a suspect discipline, as potentially a racist discipline. From my own point of view, I think we cannot ignore plausible sociobiological explanations for human behavior and we have to keep an open mind in this. Sociobiology itself is not racist; people can use sociobiological findings toward racist ends, but, as a methodology itself, it's not racist.

We've mentioned before that Darwin gave us the mechanism for human evolution, which is natural selection, natural forces acting on individuals to favor certain variants, but he didn't tell us where this variation was coming from. Darwin observed variation, but he didn't say where it was coming from. Gregor Mendel was on to the reasoning behind this, this 19th-century Moravian monk who was doing his experiments with different colored and shaped peas. His work went ignored for about 70 years, and it wasn't rediscovered until the early 1920s in a line of research that ultimately led to Watson and Crick discovering the double helix structure of DNA in 1953, and all of the changes that that has brought about.

Along with a rise in our understanding of the field of genetics, we've also developed a new approach to evolution which is called the synthetic approach, and the synthetic approach basically just combines genetics, Mendelian genetics with Darwin's theory of natural selection, explaining variation, what is the source of variation, which we know today comes from random genetic mutation and from recombination, and this provides the variation upon which natural selection acts, so it is in the new synthesis, biologists have argued, that it is the genotype rather than the phenotype, our external physical appearance which is important in evolution, and this leads us to an important modern definition for evolution: changes in gene frequencies within a population over time. We used to say that evolution was just biological change within a population over time, but now we can be more specific. We can say that it's changes in gene frequencies, and this becomes crucially important as we turn to sociobiology.

The sociobiological revolution really happened in the mid-1970s, and it started with a famous biologist named E.O. Wilson, and in 1975 he published a work called *Sociobiology: The New Synthesis*, and he was obviously playing here very self-consciously on the synthetic approach, and he was offering the new synthesis. Other people writing around the same time introduced the same ideas into the field. Richard Dawkins in particular in 1976 published a book called *The Selfish Gene*, and the ideas of sociobiology have probably been most popularized by Desmond Morris, the British scholar who gives us the sexed-up version of sociobiology. He had published a book in 1968 called *The Naked Ape*, and after all of this vocabulary of sociobiology entered the field in the mid-1970s, he became one of its most vocal and most prominent proponents. He has a number of television documentaries that are out, for example.

Now going back to E.O. Wilson, in 1975 he published *Sociobiology: The New Synthesis*, and he was a specialist in social insects, ants in particular, and he was fascinated by the behavior of ants. Why do we observe all of this sacrificial behavior on the part of worker ants? Why do they spend all of their time provisioning the queen when they could be out looking for mates themselves? Why aren't they investing all of this time and energy in reproducing themselves, in improving their own rate of reproduction? What explains this altruism, Wilson was asking, that we find among social insects? And his answer was that the workers shared their genes with the queen, and so, if they help the queen reproduce, they're actually helping reproduce their own gene pool. Now this changed the way we looked at things, not looking at an individual and the individual's reproductive success but the influence of the reproductive success of their entire gene pool.

Richard Dawkins is the one who made this most clear, and he said that individuals are just containers for genes and that we're containers for selfish genes. He says we have to stop looking at ourselves as individuals to understand human nature. What we want is not necessarily just to have a bunch of children ourselves but to pass our genes on into the next generation, and so if we help somebody who shares our genes, then we're actually helping ourselves. We're helping push our genes on into the next generation, so if we help a brother or we help a sister or we help a cousin, any of our close relatives, we're really helping ourselves. We share our genes in known proportions with our relatives: You share half of your genes with a parent; you share half of your genes with a full sibling; you share a quarter of your genes with an aunt or uncle; you share an eighth of your genes with a first cousin.

What Dawkins and Wilson were arguing, and this is the sociobiological position, that if we look at ourselves and we try and pass our genes on to the next generation, we're helping our relatives, we will help our relatives, the relatives that have a proportion of the same genes that we do. Thus it makes evolutionary sense. Let's take a hypothetical situation. You could rush into a burning house, and you would sacrifice yourself in order to save other people. A sociobiologist would say that it would be worthwhile, it would make sense for you to run into the house, if you could save three siblings or if you could save five of your aunts or uncles or if you could save nine of your cousins, because collectively that group of people would have more genes, more of your own genes than you do as an individual.

Sociobiologists say that there are certain human behaviors that are universal, that these are deep-seated propensities that have evolved way back when in what they call the environment of evolutionary adaptation, the EEA, the environment of evolutionary adaptation. Conveniently, this environment of evolutionary adaptation is more or less coequal with the Pleistocene, and that's about 1.8 million years ago to about 11,000 years ago. Human evolution, modern humans emerged about 100,000 or 200,000 years ago, so it really ends there, but for convenience's sake we can say that the environment of evolutionary adaptation is coequal with the Pleistocene. Evolutionary biologists, sociobiologists, argue that humans evolved in East Africa way back when and that we are stuck with these bodies that were adapted to the East African savanna and the East African grasslands and that the pressures that acted on us then, in these early days of evolution, continue to live on in our bodies today. Now, of course, we've developed these big brains, we have culture, we have language, we have all of these mechanisms that we can reduce the pressures of natural selection acting on us, but the sociobiologists point out we're still stuck in these bodies that are best adapted to Pleistocene East Africa, and to a degree this is certainly true.

We're predisposed to stock up on fatty foods, for example, and proteins, to eat as much sugar as we can get at any given time. This would be very adaptive again living in the Pleistocene savannas of East Africa; you have to pig out when you can because you don't know where your next meal is coming from. But in contemporary society, this predisposition has become a health problem. The newspapers are full of descriptions of the problem of obesity in modern American culture and the economic repercussions that come from this, so we have this absurdity really that's developed of diet industries, which for most of the world is crazy. Half of the world's population today lives on less than $2.00 a day; they think that paying someone to tell you to eat less and exercise more is simply absurd, but we do it, we have to do it, because we have these Pleistocene bodies stuck in this incredibly wealthy society, this affluent society where we can gorge ourselves, where we can indulge our pleasures as we see fit.

So what is fitness? What is genetic fitness? What is evolutionary fitness? We can talk about two types of fitness. The first is direct fitness, and this is really the old view of evolutionary fitness, how many children an individual has, how many of these children live to be of reproductive age and have children of their own. Indirect fitness is something that the sociobiologists began emphasizing, and indirect fitness refers to helping not only yourself, not only the number of children that an individual has, but what percentage of an individual's genes get passed on into the next generation. And by looking at indirect fitness, it leads us to what sociobiologists term kin selection, that we're much more likely to help out our close relatives than other people because they share our same genes. The sociobiologists say that we should think about inclusive fitness in addition to direct fitness, and inclusive fitness again includes not only yourself and your children but other close relatives as well.

There's a recent book by Adam Bellow called *In Defense of Nepotism*, and Adam Bellow is the son of the great contemporary American literary figure Saul Bellow, and in this book Adam Bellow argues that nepotism is really a good thing for American society, that it tempers some of the excesses of blind meritocracy. He says it's natural for humans to be nepotistic, and here he calls on sociobiological data that says that kin selection makes a lot of sense, and he argues that it's a good thing for the economy and for

American society today in that it provides some sort of long-range view. Of course, beyond the obvious irony here of Adam Bellow writing a defense of nepotism, it also seems ironic and at odds with American meritocracy, this idea that you get what you want, you become who you are in American society through your own merits and your own work.

But sociobiology was and is revolutionary because it addresses not only competition, which Darwinian theory was very good at, but it addresses cooperation as well. Why do people cooperate with each other? Is there some sort of biological basis for this? It makes sense to sacrifice yourself for your family if you can, because more of your genes can get passed down into the next generation, so the sociobiologists argue that what appears to be true altruism, what appears to be true self-sacrifice, is really self-interested behavior because we're containers for these selfish genes. Why might somebody do something sacrificial or altruistic to non-relatives? Why might a soldier, for example, throw himself on a hand grenade to save the other members of his platoon, to whom he's not related at all?

A sociobiologist would probably argue that we have this deep-seated propensity to help out our relatives, but culturally we extend who our relatives are to non-relatives at times. You may know somebody as a child that you called an aunt or an uncle, who was really just a close friend of the family, this sort of fictive kin, and among soldiers and platoons, very often they treat each other like brothers. There was that Stephen Ambrose book, *A Band of Brothers*; soldiers working together day in and day out treat themselves like siblings in some way, and so sociobiologists would argue that a soldier would be willing to throw himself on a hand grenade to save the other members of his platoon because in his mind he's thinking of them as if they were brothers of his, as if he were saving his own blood relatives and thus his own genes.

Some of the most controversial work in sociobiology has looked at the difference between men and women, the psychological and biological differences between men and women. I need to insert here another disclaimer: a number of these studies were done like psychological studies. Professors will take groups of their students in a classroom and conduct a study and then extrapolate out from those results to the rest of humanity, and so sometimes the results of these studies ring true to college-educated people in the States, for example, where they don't hold true in other cultures around the world, so we have to keep that in mind when we're talking about sociobiology.

Sociobiologists remind us that humans are an extremely K-selected species. You'll remember that there's this continuum of reproductive strategies from K to R; R-reproductive species have lots of offspring and don't invest a lot in any one of their offspring; K-selected species like humans have very few offspring and invest a lot of time and energy in the offspring that they have, and we, as humans, we give birth to these incredibly helpless infants. We have to invest a lot in our children. I was reading the other day that if humans were born at the same level of development that gorilla infants are born at, the gestation period would be 21 months long. Can you imagine a pregnancy 21 months long, giving birth to a one-year-old baby? It would be physically impossible, but that's the difference between our development. We're such a K-selected species.

Sociobiologists approach human sexual attraction and mating from an economic and evolutionary perspective. They argue that women have a window of opportunity during which they can become pregnant, and that ranges from menarche, their first menstruation, which can be in some societies as late as 17 or 18 years old—in our own society the age of first menstruation has been going down from 13 or 14 to these days about 12 years old or even younger in some cases—so the window of opportunity for pregnancies ranges from first menstruation to menopause, which happens sometime in a woman's late 40s. This varies a lot, but sometime in the late 40s. After a woman gives birth, there's a period of natural infertility.

There's some evidence here to suggest this is related to lactation; producing mother's milk releases hormones in the body that act as a natural form of birth control. So giving birth to a child, you have a nine-month gestation period, you have a period of natural infertility after birth, so it's a one- to two-year year commitment on the part of a woman to have a child, and she can only have children during this window of opportunity, from first menstruation to menopause, and even having children in the late 30s becomes biologically problematic very risky for women. You have this period of 20 to 30 years in which women can have children, and raising those children is incredibly costly, not only in our own society, where we have to pay for clothes and CDs and video games and college tuition and so forth, but even in less developed societies, if you will, it's incredibly costly to have children.

In economic terms, women have access to an incredibly valuable commodity. A woman's eggs are extremely valuable; her pregnancies are extremely valuable, and they're risky. A woman can die during childbirth. In contrast, the cost of male reproductivity approaches zero. I hate to tell you men, but the cost of sperm, the value of sperm, is virtually zero. Men produce an unlimited amount of sperm in their lifetime, and so their reproductive costs approach zero. So the sociobiologists say we've got competing intentions going on here between men and women. The women are trying to guard those pregnancies and make sure that the children are going to be cared for, that they grow up and flourish, and men can be more careless about how they spread their seed.

The sociobiologists argue that there's a point of diminishing returns here, and for women that point is reached very early. If a woman has sex with ten men and this results in one pregnancy, the other nine men, the other nine besides the one who impregnated her, are irrelevant; they're unimportant. Men, however, don't have this point of diminishing returns; a man can impregnate a virtually unlimited number of women, assuming that he has access to receptive females, so men don't have this problem of decreasing returns. Some sociobiologists—not surprisingly men here—some sociobiologists have argued that men have a genetic propensity to infidelity, an infidelity gene, if you will, and they point out that humans are not a naturally monogamous species.

Of course it's not all up to men; men don't have the only say in this. Sociobiologists would argue that men should have as much opportunistic sex as they can, that this makes mathematical sense for their reproductivity. But men have to have access to women in order to reproduce, and women thus have a very important say in who they will choose to reproduce with, and thus the women can select for certain types of males. Sociobiologists argue that females look for men who are going to be good providers, who have access to resources, money, or the possibility to make money in the future.

They're good with kids, men who are going to be willing to invest in their common offspring, make sure their kids are going to grow up and grow up right, and so women want this sort of dependability, sociobiologists argue, in a man, a commitment, a willingness to invest in children.

I was taking German classes this summer, and the teacher would throw up these slides on a screen of groups of men and women, and she would ask us to describe the people, who would we like to go out and have a cup of coffee with, for example, and we were supposed to use our adjectives here. "I would go out with the tall one or the short one" or whatever it may be, and the class is about halfway divided between men and women, and she would show pictures of groups of women to the men, and they would say things like, "I think I would like to go out and have coffee with the blond one, with the tall one or the cute one. I really like blond girls," or "I really like tall girls," or "I really like slender girls," and so forth. She would show pictures of groups of men to the women students in the class, and the women had problems with this. They would say, "Well, I don't really know who I would like to have coffee with," but then when she pressed them, they would use adjectives, but different sorts of adjectives, personality adjectives. "Well, that guy in the tweed suit looks like he would be nice. The guy in the beard looks like he would be sympathetic. That's who I would like to go and have coffee with."

We have very different criteria at work here, the men looking at external physical appearance and the women trying to get at internal personality traits, people who would be good providers for their offspring. Sociobiologists say that there are a number of things that we look for when choosing a mate, a number of things that lead us to see certain people as being attractive, and that these are biologically programmed; so the sociobiologists argue that men look for youth—that's going to indicate a longer period of potential fertility—they look for youth and fertility, and that women look for stability, access to resources, and this is often correlated with age, with being older, and so the stereotype is that men look for younger women and that women look for older men.

Sociobiologists say that we find a number of physical features naturally inherently attractive, naturally beautiful—facial symmetry for example—and there have been studies where they will take a picture of a person's face and they will digitally manipulate it. They'll cut it down the middle, and they'll create a mirror image, so we have a perfectly symmetrical face, and in studies of individuals, people almost inevitably choose the perfectly symmetrical face as more beautiful. Now why might that be? Why might we see facial symmetry as being beautiful? Sociobiologists argue that it's because it's a sign of genetic healthiness; it's an indicator that this person is genetically healthy and can have healthy offspring as well. Other symbols of such genetic healthiness that sociobiologists point to include full lips, few skin blemishes, a waist-to-hip ratio for women of 0.7, and this means having a big bust and narrow waist and then back out to have large hips, good childbearing hips. That ratio, women prefer men with a 0.9 waist-to-hip ratio, which is like an inverted triangle.

A lot of these sociobiological explanations hold true for American college students at least, maybe for large portions of American society, but we can find counterexamples in various cultures around the world. We studied attractiveness, for example, among Andean populations in Peru and Bolivia and they don't find the hourglass figure that's supposed to be inherently attractive to human males, Andean men don't find this attractive at all. They prefers short, squat, sort of square-figured women, and one could argue that this is adaptive for the environment that they live in, this harsh, high-altitude environment with extremely cold temperatures, so sturdier women perhaps are better adapted, but it derides the sociobiological explanation that this is a universal human propensity. Think back in our own culture, in Western culture, think back to the pictures of Rubens or Titian, or any of these other painters who painted these voluptuous women who today we would consider to be slightly overweight at best.

Sociobiologists argue that women are trying to get men to commit. It's in men's best interest to commit very often because they'll have a sure thing. They can make sure it makes economic, biological, economic, evolutionary sense to have a single partner, to be in a monogamous relationship, to ensure that the children are going to be raised well and to survive and reach reproductive age themselves. However, sociobiologists also argue that men have this infidelity gene, this metaphorical infidelity gene that encourages them not only to have the sure thing at home but to seek out opportunistic sex as well. What the sociobiologists ignore in all of this is the power of culture, the power of culture in changing the way in which people live and work.

Take celibate priests, for example. Sociobiologists have a really hard time explaining why we have celibate priests, and there's been a lot of news lately about priests who are not celibate, and yet the vast majority of them remain celibate. How does a sociobiologist account for that? What reproductive sense does that make? They can't, and so what the sociobiologists, I think they have a lot to offer us in terms of basic propensities that are built into the human condition, perhaps evolving in this environment of evolutionary adaptation, but they miss that culture trumps biology very often.

Lecture Six
Languages, Dialects, and Social Categories

Scope:

Language is an element of existence that makes us human: The fact that we have language, that we can communicate with each other, gives rise to culture and sets us apart from other animals. It is unclear when language first arose among our ancestors (perhaps as early as 300,000 or as recently as 100,000 years ago), but writing came along only about 6,000 years ago. All humans have a language, but languages vary greatly around the world. It seems that mental maps of a language's particular sounds are laid down early in life and are incredibly resilient; the older one becomes, the harder it is to master the phonology and grammar of another tongue. Linguists study how people communicate; this involves not just syntax and grammar, but also body language and facial expressions. The linguist Charles Hockett proposes a list of features that make human language unique. These include the ability to say totally new things and to talk about events not in the present. However, recent work with apes has shown that many capabilities we have thought were uniquely human are shared among higher primates.

Language certainly tells us a lot about the speaker, not just the words spoken but how they are said. Dialects, for example, are important markers of one's social origins, and a number of studies have shown that speaking a particular dialect calls into play a whole host of stereotypes and preconceptions.

Outline

I.   Humans are both united and divided by language.

    A. Although spoken language has been around for at least 100,000 years, written languages are relatively recent.

    B. Languages vary greatly in their particulars, but there are a few important common elements.

        1. All languages have a grammar (whether it is written or not) and are wholly functioning systems.

        2. Languages are constantly changing.

II. Technical linguistics looks at the structures of languages.

    A. Spoken language is based on sounds, or *phonemes*.

    B. Written languages imperfectly represent phonemes.

        1. In *logographic* writing systems, symbols are used to represent units of meanings (and, sometimes, whole words).

        2. *Syllabic* and *alphabetic* systems combine a smaller number of symbols ("letters") to represent the sounds of words.

    C. Phonemes are combined to create *morphemes* (the minimal units of meaning in a language); morphemes combine to create words; and words combine in a way prescribed by syntax and grammar.

        1. All languages have a grammar.

        2. Noam Chomsky has suggested that there is an innate capacity for the mind to produce grammar.

    D. Linguists have also discovered that a great deal of what we communicate occurs nonverbally.

        1. As much as 80 percent of the meaning conveyed in a conversation may come from body language (*kinesics*).

        2. *Proxemics* is the study of the physical distance between speakers, showing how notions of personal space vary between cultures.

III. The ability to produce language is a hallmark feature of the human condition, giving rise to the unique cognitive and cultural capabilities of the species.

    A. Most scientists agree that language is uniquely human, but there has been great disagreement on what exactly this means. The linguist Charles Hocket proposed a number of features that, combined, make language human.

        1. Language is an *open system*, as opposed to the closed call systems of other animals. This is to say that human language is infinitely variable, not confined to a few predetermined signals.

        2. Human language exhibits *displacement*, the ability to talk about the past, the future, and things not immediately present.

3. The words used by human languages are arbitrary representations. This builds on Ferdinand de Saussure's observation that a sign (such as a word) is composed of a *signifier* (the combination of sounds that make up a word) and the *signified* (the actual object, idea, or person referred to).

B. Studies with apes have shown that with intensive training, apes can be taught rudimentary language skills.

1. The most famous "talking apes" are Washoe the chimp and Koko the gorilla. Both learned a variant of American Sign Language.

2. Washoe and Koko have proven that apes can use language productively; that they can discuss distant events (displacement); and that they can even lie (prevarication having been thought to be uniquely human).

3. Nonetheless, apes never reach beyond a two- to three-year level of language mastery, even after years of training.

IV. The language one speaks, and the way one speaks it, carries a good deal of information about one's background and social class.

A. The linguist Max Weinreich famously defined a language as a dialect with a navy, meaning that language distinctions are politically loaded and often privilege dominant cultures.

1. A *dialect* is commonly defined as a mutually intelligible variety of a language, but often, it is difficult to know where exactly to draw the line.

2. As languages are not easily mastered, and dialects hard to eschew, the way one speaks acts as a good indicator of identity and class.

B. Different dialects carry different prestige values and are often used in the exercise of power.

1. In Spanish, French, German, and many languages, one uses two sets of pronouns, one familiar and the other more formal. Such pronouns require speakers to constantly acknowledge social distance in communication.

2. William Labov has studied the pronunciation of a final *r* following a vowel between social classes in New York City.
3. Speakers who have mastered two dialects often switch back and forth, depending on social context.
4. Controversies exist over how much a dialect should be valued, such as with black vernacular English (Ebonics) in the United States.

Readings:

Steven Pinker, *The Language Instinct*.

Edward T. Hall, *The Silent Language*.

Internet Resources:

http://www.koko.org/. The Gorilla Foundation.

Questions to Consider:

1. How does human language differ from animal call systems?
2. What does the use of a particular dialect tell us about the speaker?
3. What are the politics of dialect and language distinctions?

Lecture Six—Transcript
Languages, Dialects, and Social Categories

Language is something that makes us human. We have language so we can communicate with each other, and not just facts, but ideas, hopes, dreams, emotions, theories. It's what allows culture; language allows culture. Most of what we know about culture, indeed most of what we know at all, comes to us through language, so in this lecture we're going to look at just exactly what language is and what it is not, what are its components. We'll talk about the sounds of language, alphabets, grammars, what sets it apart from other forms of animal communication and what do we have to learn from chimps and apes who have learned variants of language. We're going to conclude today by looking at dialects as markers of identity and how one speaks can tell a lot about who one is.

We don't know when language first arose among our ancestors. The physical remains that would tell us about this are mostly soft tissue, like vocal chords, and they don't last very long in the archaeological record, but at some point our larynx falls, creating our Adam's apple and allowing us to produce the vast range of sounds that we need to speak. There are dangers in this as well. When the larynx falls, it also allows us to choke on our own food, so there had to be some huge evolutionary benefit to allowing our larynx to fall, and that evolutionary benefit is spoken language. This first occurred maybe 300,000 years ago, maybe 100,000 years ago. We're not really sure because the tissues don't remain in the archaeological record. Writing, this is important to note, writing only comes along about 6,000 years ago. Most languages in the world were not written and are not written.

We do know that if language is not learned early on, it cannot be fully mastered, so we have this biological capacity to produce language. But if we don't learn a language early in life, we'll probably never learn it, and we can see this in the very few cases we have documented of feral children. In 17th-, 18th-, 19th-century Europe, there would occasionally be these children found that were raised in the wild by wolves or whatever it may be, and they never fully mastered language, so if they didn't learn it from a very early age they could never master it in later life.

Language is a system of communication. It is one of the great rules of languages that, like culture, it's always changing. Languages are always changing. There are about 6,000 languages spoken in the world today, although they're dying out fast, actually. There may be as few as half of that in 100 years' time, by some estimates. Following European contact in the new world, for example, the number of native languages fell by half, and very quickly. Languages are always changing. Languages are also all fundamentally equal. If a speaker of any language has something that they want to say, they can communicate that idea, so languages are all fundamentally equal in that way as well.

Some languages have a larger vocabulary than others in certain domains. Technology in English, for example, we have this huge vocabulary of technological words that some other languages don't have, but when those languages need to refer to that computer or to that software, or whatever it may be, they come up with a word. In Kaqchikel Maya, the language in which I worked, for example, until not long ago there was one word, *ch'ich*, for all metal things—it could be a typewriter; it could be a bus. If it was metal it was called *ch'ich*, but today, as more Maya are becoming educated, as more Maya are participating in the modern economy, they have elaborate vocabularies, not only for cars and typewriters but for computers and software, so when there's a need for someone to say something, when there's a need for language to communicate an idea, that language can always be flexible enough to meet it.

Anthropological linguists work mostly with undescribed languages, undocumented languages, and a lot of what they do is writing dictionaries, writing grammars, recording these languages for posterity. In describing languages—technical linguistics, we can call it—we can break this down into several different components, the most fundamental of which are sounds, different sounds and languages. I would like to introduce two vocabulary terms here, *phonemics* and *phonetics*. Phonemics refers to the sounds that a native speaker hears. Phonetics refers to the more objective qualities of the sound waves. You remember early on, we made this distinction between emic and etic, emic being the view from within the culture, and this comes from phonemic, and phonetic gives rise to etic, the more objective, the more scientific, the outside view.

Just as we learn to divide up the color spectrum into meaningful segments—red, yellow, green, blue and so forth—we also learn to break up the sound spectrum into meaningful segments as well, A, E, I, O, and U, and these are culturally specific. There are very few cultural universals in terms of language; all languages, for example, distinguish between vowels and consonants. But beyond that, there's a huge range of variation, and not every language recognizes the same sounds. In Japanese, for example, they don't recognize the difference phonemically, from within the culture, between Rs and Ls, something that sounds very distinct to an English speaker, but for a Japanese speaker it doesn't sound very distinct. In Spanish, we find the same thing with V and B; they don't really hear this distinction, and so it's very hard when they learn English that makes a clear distinction between V and B. In my own dialect—I'm from the south; I grew up in Alabama—in my own dialect of English, we refer to this as a pen [pronounced pin], the same word that we would use for the sewing instrument, a pin. We sew with a pin, and I write with a pen. In many dialects of English, there would be a clear phonetic distinction between those two sounds.

There are also tonal languages, and in tonal languages the inflection changes the meaning of a word, and the most famous example comes from Chinese, which is a tonal language, where the word which is transcribed in English *ma*—we would pronounce as ma—can mean four different things. You can say ma, which is mother; you can say ma, which is linen; you could say ma, which is horse; or you could say ma, which is scold. Depending on how just this one-syllable word is inflected, it changes the difference, and lots of students of Chinese, English speakers learning Chinese, have said things like, "My horse and my father and my brothers and sisters, we all live together in one happy family." These tonal differences are very hard for native English speakers, for example, to learn; if you don't learn these sound differences early on in life, they're very hard to pick up later on.

Another interesting phonetic structure we find in sub-Saharan languages called click languages, and here there are a number of sounds, clicking sounds. For example, you have [click click], you have [click click], sounds like this that are difficult. English speakers can make these sounds, but it's very difficult to put them in a word. Try and put these sounds in the middle of a word, and our tongues just can't seem to wrap around it. So if you don't hear the sounds of a language before the age of six, maybe seven, maybe eight, and maybe as late as 12 years old, you can never fully internalize the phonetic maps of these other languages.

Most languages, as I said, are unwritten. Written languages are really the exception rather than the rule, although we associate writing with language these days, but in terms of written languages there are three main types, and these are logographic, meaning that one sign stands for a word or an idea; syllabic, a sign stands for a syllable; or alphabetic, like our own system. In logographic systems, the problem is, you have to have an immense number of characters to represent all of the words in the language. Let's take Chinese again as an example. Chinese is commonly called a logographic language, although actually it's a combination of logographic and phonetic elements. Chinese has 1,300 logographic components; it's an incredible barrier for people trying to learn this language. The benefit to this is that speakers of Cantonese and Mandarin though can look at the same symbol and pronounce it in their own language, so it's not as closely tied to the sound patterns.

Syllabic languages first arose with the Phoenicians. Mayan hieroglyphs are syllabic, for example, and they represent a vowel-consonant combination, with one sign, and English famously is alphabetical. It's alphabetic, only 26 characters; we have 26 characters in our alphabet to represent the whole range of words and sounds that we can make, so alphabetic systems are much more flexible and much more streamlined in this manner, although there's always a slippage between the alphabetic sign, not always but there can be, slippage between the alphabetic sign and the sounds that it produces. My five-year-old daughter, for example, thinks that *car* is spelled with a K, and we learn over time when to pronounce a C as a K and when to pronounce it as an S sound. We learn all of these variants, but it's not necessarily given in the alphabetic character itself.

Linguists study phonetic differences and phonemic differences between languages. They study how these phonemes are combined to create morphemes, and morphemes are the minimal units of meaning, usually a word, but it doesn't have to be a word. Bike is a morpheme, but if we add an S to that, bikes, it becomes a two-morpheme word, so linguists look at how phonemes are combined to create morphemes, how morphemes are combined to create words, and how words are combined through the rules of syntax and grammar. Grammar is basically the rules of the language, how you put words together to make meaningful sentences. All languages have a grammar; not all languages have a *Little Brown Handbook*, not all languages have a *Chicago Manual of Style*, not all languages have a written grammar, but all languages have a grammar.

These grammars differ rather dramatically. If you've ever tried to learn German or Chinese, you'll appreciate the vast differences in grammars in different languages, but functionally they're equal, and this gets back to a point that we made earlier in the lecture, that any language can communicate any idea, so functionally grammars all serve the same purpose, creating common rules that everybody can understand in order to facilitate communication. The linguist Noam Chomsky has argued that humans are not only born with a capacity for language but really what he calls a black box in the brain which produces grammar, and he says that there is some sort of proto-grammar that's innate in human brains. Is grammar innate? I'm not sure. Do humans have an innate capacity for language? Most certainly. The language that humans learn, however, is precisely that: it's what they learn; it's not given at birth in any way.

So linguists study phonetics, they study grammar. Linguists also study semantics, the meanings of words, not just the dictionary meanings but the subtle shades of meanings that particular words can carry. For language to work, there has to be some fundamental agreement about what words mean. Right? This is the whole purpose of communication; we all agree what certain words mean. But a lot of times there's slippage here as well. Take, for example, have you ever had the experience of using a word perhaps frequently and then discovering that you don't really know what it means? You may have read it in a newspaper, you read it in a book, you intuited the meaning of the word from the context, and then it turns out later that that's not really the word, but it suited you very well to use it in your own particular idiosyncratic way, so these sort of things happen all the time.

We have phonetics, we have grammar, we have semantics, the meanings of words, but linguists have also been turning recently to the study of body language, and they point out that a lot of what we communicate actually happens nonverbally. In some studies, they estimate that as much as 80 percent of the information communicated happens nonverbally, and this can happen in a variety of ways through body language, which we call kinesics, body language. Do you speak to someone with your arms folded or do you speak to someone with your arms open? What sorts of subtle signs are you giving to the people that you're communicating with? One interesting thing that I read not long ago is that if you raise your eyebrows, and we subconsciously do this when we meet somebody, or when you see somebody that you like a lot, you unconsciously raise your eyebrows, and so we can use these things to manipulate social situations as well. Next time you meet somebody, raise your eyebrows and see if the interaction happens any differently.

So body language, a lot is communicated by body language, a lot is communicated by proxemics, how we stand in relation to the person that we're communicating with. In the U.S., we have a fairly big comfort bubble. We need to have two or four feet between us and a person that we're having a casual conversation with. In other cultures around the world, that comfort bubble is much smaller, and if you've ever traveled, if you've traveled in Latin America, for example, you may feel uncomfortable when everybody comes up and puts their arms around you and touches you in a way that we would consider to be very intimate, but for them it's just a natural way of showing their friendship and their appreciation. This can result in a sort of ballet in certain situations.

There was a study done of different banks in New York City, and this graduate student went to a really WASP bank, a really white bank, where all of the clientele were white, and then she went to a bank in an Italian neighborhood in New York City, and what she would do is she would stand in the teller line and she would get gradually closer to the person in front of her, and when she was at this WASP bank, she would basically end up chasing these patrons around the bank. As she got closer, they would move away, and she would get closer and they would move away still, and then when she went to the bank in the Italian neighborhood, she could practically be hugging the person in front of her and they wouldn't move, so there was this very different cultural sense of space and what's appropriate.

We can apply this to all sorts of things, office design, how our office is designed, what is the height of the chair of the person behind the desk and the person in front of the desk, for example. In my office at my university, I have a chair that's very, very low that students sit in, and I sit in a normal chair, and this creates this very subtle power differential between us. So there are all sort of ways in which proxemics can facilitate, often in subtle ways, but facilitate communication and communicate lots of ideas. So that's the basic overview of what linguists do.

But I'd like to talk to you specifically about language and what language is. We generally consider language to be uniquely human. This is something that only humans have, is language, but what is then language? The linguist Charles Hockett tried to come up with a list of features that define language as uniquely human. He came up with a total of about 13, although I'm only going to go over a few here today. Hockett argues that language is one—it's an open system; it's not a closed system. Chimpanzee communication is what we call a call system; they can only say a limited number of things. Bees can communicate, but they can only say a limited number of things. In human language, we can say an infinite number of things. It's an open system; it's productive. We routinely make up entirely new constructions. Think of some of the great literary figures in the world: James Joyce. Reading *Ulysses*, this is so difficult because he's really using the productivity of language, putting words together in a totally new way, or Allen Ginsberg's *Howl*. We can all think of literary pioneers in this way. Language is an open system; it's not a closed system.

The second feature is displacement. Human language can talk about things that are not in the here and now. We can talk about the past; we can make up fictions; we can talk about our hopes and dreams for tomorrow and the future. Animal closed systems can't do this. And it's a fundamental feature of human languages. We can teach a dog to bark on a certain command, but we can't teach that dog to bark tomorrow if it's raining, for example, so there's a fundamental limitation in closed systems and other forms of communication in terms of displacement. Third, we have arbitrariness, that language is arbitrary. The symbol and sound combination that we use, that we link together in language, is arbitrary. You can call this furry, four-legged creature a dog; you can call it a hound in Germany; you could call it a perro in Spanish. All of these are perfectly good words and we just agree that we're going to use those words to refer to this object, but there's an arbitrary relationship there.

There's not a natural relationship between the words that we use and what is denoted by those. This is something that was actually given to us by Ferdinand de Saussure, the father of scientific linguistics, of modern linguistics, and he said that we can divide signs up into two components. In a sign, you have the signifier, and that could be a symbol, it could be a word, it can be a written word, it can be a spoken word, and then you have the signified, and the signified is the thing that is being referred to, and Saussure, one of his important contributions was to make this distinction, that there's an arbitrary relationship between the signifier, the word that we use, and the signified, the object that we're referring to. Can you think of any exceptions? When I ask my students, most of the time they say, "Well, what about onomatopoetic words? What about animal sounds?" Even here, if you studied foreign languages, you'll know that even here foreign languages have different sounds for different animals. In Spanish, for example, a rooster says *kikiriki*, whereas in English it says *cockle-doodle-doo*, so even onomatopoetic words share this quality of arbitrariness.

Studies with apes have shown that with intensive training apes, chimpanzees, and gorillas can be taught rudimentary language skills, and here I'd like to mention two in particular. The first is Washoe, and this was a chimp who was trained first at the University of Nevada and then moved to the University of Oklahoma, and work was done with Washoe in the 1960s. She was taught a modified version of American Sign Language. They worked with her for about four years, and, all in all, she learned 150 different signs and could communicate basic ideas, so we have Washoe, the chimp, and Koko. Koko, the gorilla, now lives in a foundation in California. Koko was born in 1971. She was first in the San Francisco Zoo and then she was taken for research at this private foundation, and researchers have worked with Koko for over 25 years, also teaching her a modified version of American Sign Language, and she now has a vocabulary of over 1,000 words.

I bring this up at this point because work with these apes has made us question some of Hockett's list of what is distinctly human about language. Let's take productivity, first of all, that we can produce totally new linguistic phrases to encompass new ideas. We find this among these apes. Washoe, for example, when she first saw a fur coat, called it a hair coat. This seems pretty basic, a hair coat, but she took two words that she knew previously from other contexts and put them together to describe something that she'd never seen before. She was being productive in her language use. The first time she saw a candy bar she called it a sweet banana, again using two words that she had known before and putting them together in a different way. We've also seen productivity with Koko, the gorilla. The first time, Koko was out on a field trip one day and saw a duck for the first time and signed to his trainer "water bird," and the trainers just went crazy because, again, a sign of productive speech.

Let's take displacement. Koko's erstwhile mate, companion, recently died, was Michael, another gorilla that was captured in the wild as an infant. It was captured while it was an infant in Vienna, and eventually mated to this foundation in California, and at one point Koko taught Michael a lot of signs. The trainers also taught Michael a lot of signs, and at one point he described seeing his mother being killed, and it's assumed that his mother was killed by poachers and that as an infant he was taken away and sold, but this describes displacement. He was able to talk about something not in the here and now, something way back when, displacement.

So Hockett and others started adding to this list of features that make language uniquely human. Language has to be uniquely human, so let's add to this list of features, and one thing they added was prevarication, lying. Only in human language can you lie, but actually we've seen evidence of this as well. Koko, unbeknownst to her, was filmed all the time, 24 hours a day, a little video camera in the corner of her, you can't really call it a cage—she really lives in a room—and one night she broke her feeding bowl, and the next morning her trainer comes in and says, "What happened to the bowl?" and she signs back, "The other trainer did it," and she didn't realize that she was being filmed, but she lied. She lied because she was embarrassed about what had happened.

We've also seen in the wild—we have evidence of lying among chimpanzees in the wild. Chimpanzees have been seen to find a slaughtered animal, let's say an antelope that a lion has killed, eaten part of and then left, and sometimes chimpanzees will call out a warning signal to the rest of their troop, saying, "Watch out, there's a lion in the area." Everybody leaves, all the other chimps leave. This chimp comes down, gorges on the antelope meat and then presumably comes back to the troop later and says, "Yeah, that lion just left. I don't know what happened to him." We find lying, we find displacement, we find productivity, all of these among apes who have learned variants of American Sign Language. Nonetheless, Koko, Washoe, the other apes who have been studied this way, they never get beyond the vocabulary of a three- or four- or maybe a five-year-old human. They never reach beyond a few hundred words. Koko is the most, with a thousand-word vocabulary today, so it's still very limited, but they do share some of these characteristics with human languages.

There are 6,000 languages spoken in the world today. The most widely spoken are Mandarin Chinese, Hindu, English, and Spanish. English is by far the most widely spoken language if we include second-language speakers as well for whom English is a second language. In some places, especially where there are dramatic ecological geographic barriers to communication between communities, we find high densities of different languages. For example, in Highland New Guinea, there are hundreds, perhaps as many as 900 different languages spoken in this little area of Highland New Guinea because the geography is so grand. One community couldn't communicate very effectively with the community on the other side of the hill, and so over time they develop distinctive variants. In Guatemala, where I work with the Maya, there are 21 separate Mayan languages spoken, not dialects, languages, 21 languages spoken, and this is in a country smaller than the size of the state of Tennessee.

But what is a language and what is a dialect? Languages, if one speaks a different language, it implies mutual unintelligibility. You cannot understand what the other person is saying. In contrast, a dialect implies mutual intelligibility. It's a variant of the language, but we can still understand what is being said, and the variations can be phonemic, they can be grammatical, they can be in terms of vocabulary intonation, body language. We can have all sorts of dialectical variations. Language is not mutually intelligible from others, but there are a lot of gradations here. Swedish and

Norwegian, for example, are considered to be separate languages, and yet among good-willed speakers they can understand each other, but there's this whole history of political conflict between the two countries that leads them to establish themselves or promote themselves as being two separate languages.

Spanish and Portuguese, a bit greater distance there, but again among good-willed speakers. I'm a pretty good speaker of Spanish, and I can follow a basic Portuguese conversation, and so where is that line then between a separate language and a dialect? We often speak of the Chinese language, but of course there are many Chinese languages, Mandarin and Cantonese, for example, and it's a very powerful political statement to talk about the Chinese language, grouping all of these heterogeneous groups together as a single entity. The linguist Max Wienreich famously defined a language as a dialect with a navy. A language is a dialect with a navy, and what he was getting at here is that language distinctions are really very often political distinctions as well. It's not based on science.

There is a science to this to distinguish between a dialect and a language, and the way in which we do this is judging the percentage of cognates, and cognate words, or words that have the same root or can be recognized as being the same cognates—hound in English and hound in Germany for example—so we can look at the percentage of cognates between two languages or two dialects and we can create a cutoff point. For example, if these two variants have less than 70 percent shared cognates, they're separate languages, or we could say 80 percent, or we could say 90 percent. But at some point we can draw a line and say this is a separate language and not just a dialectical variation. But where do we draw the line? It seems very scientific to use percentages like that, but where do we draw that line? It ultimately becomes arbitrary. Is 70 percent a common vocabulary? Is that a different language, 80 percent? 90 percent? Who knows?

Languages and dialects can serve as very powerful identity markers. Languages are not easily learned; they're not easily shirked off—we don't lose a language very easily—so they can serve as powerful symbols of a person's cultural heritage, and we use them this way. In English, take English English, British English, a public school dialect versus a commoner dialect. This tells a lot about a person; the way in which the person speaks tells a lot about that person. In English, we refer to Standard English as SAE, American English, Standard American English, this non-descript, Midwestern dialect of standard American English, and this is the most highly valued form of English in the United States. A number of studies have been done showing that people have prejudices against those with strong Southern accents, strong Northeastern accents. Any sort of strong accent invokes a number of stereotypes about the person who is speaking.

One interesting study was done by the linguist William Labov, who went around to different department stores in New York City looking at whether the final "r" in a word was pronounced, if people would pronounce the final "r" in "floor," for example, and he found that at Saks Fifth Avenue, all of the shoppers and all of the storekeepers would pronounce this final "r," and he said that this was a sign of a certain socio-economic status, a high status. He found at Klein's, a much lower-priced department store in New York City, that hardly anybody pronounced this "r," again an indicator of socio-economic status. We could talk about black vernacular English, also encompassing lots of stereotypes about how people speak and about who they are.

We've looked at a great diversity of language. Even if Noam Chomsky argues that there's a common foundational grammar, there's a great diversity of languages spoken in the world, but we communicate not only with words but with body language as well. Not only what we say but how we say it, our language, our dialect, tells a lot about our social identity and about our politics in cases as well. While the capacity for language may be innate, its realization is always a unique, creative, productive process.

Lecture Seven
Language and Thought

Scope:

Can you think of something that you cannot put into words? To what extent is thought determined by language? The linguist Benjamin Lee Whorf argues that linguistic structures actually determine the way we look at the world. He asserts that the way Hopi grammar treats verb tenses, for example, results in what whites perceive as a lackadaisical attitude toward time. In a similar vein, scholars have shown how American men and women speak subtly different varieties of English (resulting in much miscommunication) and how common metaphors in American English (such as "time is money") shape the way we think about the world around us.

The way we talk to one another—our discourse strategies—shapes and reflects our social relationships. In this light, discourse analysis uncovers the often hidden power structures encoded in everyday speech.

Outline

I. The Sapir-Whorf hypothesis posits that language structures the way we look at the world.

   A. Benjamin Lee Whorf (1897–1941), a part-time linguist and fire insurance investigator, conducted influential work to examine how language structures influence thought.

      1. In a wonderful piece titled "Blazing Icicles," he shows how semantic misunderstandings led to a number of easily preventable fires.

      2. He also proposed that Hopi conceptions of time (not as linear and rigid as ours) have led to their characterization as "lazy Indians," unable to keep to a schedule.

   B. Whorf studied linguistics under Edward Sapir and took his inspiration from Sapir's writings about language.

      1. The line of thought he developed has come to be known as the *Sapir-Whorf hypothesis*, and it has two main variants.

2. The strong version of the Sapir-Whorf hypothesis (or the linguistic determinism approach) posits that linguistic structures (vocabulary and grammar) determine the way one can think.

3. The weak version (or linguistic relativity) holds simply that linguistic categories and structures influence thought (and are, in turn, influenced by it).

4. The context in which languages arise necessitates certain vocabulary differences—Inuit have many words for *snow*; the Bedouins many words for *sand*.

5. In Mayan languages, certain numerical classifiers are grammatically required, which may influence worldview.

II. Research on metaphors and discourse strategies shows the real-world implications of language use.

A. Recent research by linguist Deborah Tannen has found a number of gender-specific forms of speech.

1. Women tend to speak more indirectly, asking rather than commanding and hedging many of their assertions.

2. Such indirect speech is associated with women but often employed by men as well.

3. Flight recorder data from a 1982 Air Florida crash shows how indirect speech may have devastating effects.

B. George Lakoff and Mark Johnson argue, in *Metaphors We Live By*, that certain core metaphors in American English structure the way we think about the world.

1. One key metaphor is "time is money," in which time is treated as a valuable commodity, an object that can be spent, wasted, saved, invested, and so on.

2. "Argument is war" is another salient metaphor that shapes the way we argue and think about argument.

III. Discourse analysis examines real speech as used in particular contexts. We all use—often unknowingly—a number of discourse strategies and shortcuts.

A. But language is not simply enacting scripts—we use language actively and creatively. In this light, it is useful to look for broad strategies that individuals employ in their interactions.

B. Presuppositions are a powerful rhetorical tool and may be used to mark in-group versus out-group (with a private joke, for example) or establish social distance.

    1. To save face, we often employ varieties of pre-invitations—subtly checking to see if an invitation would be accepted before proffering it (e.g., "What are you doing Saturday night?").

    2. Examining turn-taking in a conversation can reveal a lot about the power dynamics between the individuals.

Readings:

Benjamin Whorf, *Language, Thought, and Reality.*

George Lakoff and Mark Johnson, *Metaphors We Live By.*

Deborah Tannen, *You Just Don't Understand: Women and Men in Conversation.*

Questions to Consider:

1. How do men and women speak differently? Is this a serious barrier to communication?

2. How can the categories given by our language mold the way we think about things?

3. How much of our daily speech is scripted and how much is improvised?

Lecture Seven—Transcript
Language and Thought

As we said last time, the language and dialect we speak can tell others a lot about who we are, and this is a symbolic quality, independent of what's being said. In fact, it might overshadow what's being said in certain contexts, but language, of course, also serves as a vehicle for communication, and so in this lecture we're going to look at the relationship between languages, how we communicate, and thought, what we want to communicate. Can you think of something that you cannot say? Can you think of something that you can't put into words? If so, the responses that I normally give are that it's an emotion, "I'm so mad I can't speak," "I'm so in love with you that words escape me," or perhaps it's a visual or an auditory impression, a painting or a piece of music that touches you in ways that are impossible to fully articulate.

But given these exceptions, to a large extent, our language does mediate our thought. We don't simply express ourselves through language; we also think through language in many ways. Language gives us the categories, the vocabularies, the verb structure and so on that frame not only how we talk but how we perceive the world. We see green where other cultures might see blue because of the linguistic category that we've constructed called green. In this lecture, we examine the ways in which language influences thought. We're going to look specifically at the Sapir-Whorf hypothesis and the ways we construct ourselves and present themselves linguistically, such as in men's and women's speech, and the role of metaphors in the way in which we look at the world.

I'd like to begin by discussing the work of Benjamin Lee Whorf. He was born in 1897; he died in 1941. He got his degree from the Massachusetts Institute of Technology, a B.S. in chemical engineering in 1918. After graduation, he went to work for the Hartford Fire Insurance Company as a trainee and fire prevention engineer, and after graduation he kept up with his interest in linguistics, so he studied on his own. He studied Hebrew; he studied Nahuatl, the language of the Aztecs. He studied Maya; he even traveled to southern Mexico to look at Mayan cliffs. And he took a few classes from Edward Sapir at Yale, and Sapir was a student of Boas's. Whorf remained with the Hartford Fire Insurance Company for the rest of his short life, developing a national reputation as an expert in industrial fire prevention.

He authored several articles on fire prevention, including one titled "Blazing Icicles," and this offered a linguistic interpretation of fire prevention; it's probably the most readable fire prevention report ever written. He looked at a couple of case studies in particular. At one, there was a warehouse that had burned down in a fire, and so he goes and investigates, and he finds out that what they would do is, they used in their production process, they used gas, and they would take empty containers and put them on the loading dock, and they were labeled as empty gas containers. On the same loading dock is where the workers would come out and take their breaks, and one day a worker was out taking a break, smoking a cigarette, and flipped his cigarette into these empty gas containers, which promptly blew up of course and burned down the building.

Now what Whorf said was that the seeds of this disaster lay in the semantics of empty. Empty means both without its usual contents and null and void or inert. Here these gas containers were without their usual contents. They weren't filled up with liquid gas, but they were all the more dangerous because of that, because an empty gas can is actually full of gas vapors, which are more flammable than the liquid gas was in the first place, and so it was a linguistic, a semantic slip, that allowed for this disaster to take place. He looked at a couple of other instances like this, instances of inflammable, labels saying inflammable being confused, because it's a very confusing word. Inflammable means flammable; it throws us off because this in-prefix usually means a negation, inconsistent, incoherent, so why inflammable? He showed that it led to a number of fire disasters.

Spun limestone, he gave another example of a factory that used spun limestone that people would treat very carelessly because it was stone, it's limestone, but actually this particular product, spun limestone, when it's heated up produces acetone, which is very volatile, can catch fire very easily, and so he was looking in "Blazing Icicles" at these cases where linguistic misunderstandings led to fire disasters. The categories employed by a language, he argued, determined the way in which people looked at the world. The words these workers were using influenced their behavior and led to these disasters. This line of thought that he developed has come to be known as the Sapir-Whorf hypothesis. It's probably more accurate to call it the Whorfian hypothesis; he took a sentence from a book written by Edward Sapir and expanded on that and made this whole theoretical structure.

The Sapir-Whorf hypothesis, or the Whorfian hypothesis, if you will, says that the structure of a language determines cognition. The way we think about the world, and thus culture, is given to us by the structures of our language. The Sapir-Whorf hypothesis has two main variants. We can talk about the strong version and the weak version. The strong version of the Sapir-Whorf hypothesis, also called linguistic determinism, posits that linguistic structures, vocabulary and grammar, determine the way in which one can think. The strong version, linguistic structures determine the way in which one can think. Probably the best example of this comes to us from literature, in George Orwell's novel *1984* and the language Newspeak, which was developed to enforce the ideology of the society that Orwell described in *1984*. Let me read just a short passage here because it illustrates so nicely the strong version of the Sapir-Whorf hypothesis.

"The purpose of Newspeak was not only to provide a medium of expression for the world view and mental habits proper to the devotees of Insoc, but to make all other modes of thought impossible. A thought diverging from the principles of Insoc should be literally unthinkable, at least so far as thought is dependent on words." Its vocabulary was so constructed as to give exact and often very subtle expression to every meaning that a party member could properly wish to express while excluding all other means, language determining thought in this case, the strong version of the Sapir-Whorf hypothesis. The weak version of the Sapir-Whorf hypothesis, which is much more palatable and is also called linguistic relativity, holds simply that there is a relationship between language and thought, that language influences the way in which we think and that the way in which we think influences language. This weak version is the most accepted version; it still doesn't resolve this chicken and egg question, however, of what comes first, thought or words.

Now Whorf used a couple of different lines of evidence to support his hypothesis, and the first came from vocabulary. He famously noted that Eskimos have more words for types of snow than English speakers do, and he deduced that therefore Eskimos must perceive of snow differently. This is an example that has come to take on apocryphal proportions in anthropology. Sometimes you'll read in introductory textbooks that there are 100 different Eskimo words for snow, this word that we only have a single word for in English. We can trace this back, however, to the work of Franz Boas, and in 1911 he published *The Handbook of North American Indians* and he noted that Eskimos have four different words for snow, where English just had one.

The Eskimo have *aput*, means on the ground; *gana*, falling snow; *piqsirpoq*, drifting snow; or *qimuqsuq* for a snowdrift. In English, we can make these decisions, but we need a phrase to make a distinction, where Eskimo just have the one word, so Whorf latches onto this idea that he read in Boas's booked and then takes off with it, and he publishes an article in 1940 called "Science and Linguistics," and let me quote from him here. He writes, "We have the same word for falling snow, snow on the ground, snow packed hard like ice, slushy snow, wind-driven flying snow, whatever the situation may be. To an Eskimo, this all-inclusive word would be almost unthinkable. He would say that falling snow, slushy snow, and so on are sensuously and operationally different, different things to contend with. He uses different words for them and for other kinds of snow."

You'll notice here that he's taken Boas's observation that there are four Eskimo words for snow and sort of made it a little bit more nebulous, so it sounds like there are more than four words for snow. There's been a lot of controversy in anthropological linguistics about this. Exactly how many Eskimo words for snow are there? It turns out that the Eskimo have certain prefixes and suffixes that can make words look like different words when they're actually just variants of the same word. One linguist that I read not long ago estimates that, in fact, there are probably about 12 to15 words in the Inuit language for snow, and in fact this isn't so different from English. Think of English words for snow: avalanche; blizzard; a dusting; a flurry; frost; hail; hard-packed snow. We have a fairly extensive vocabulary as well, although it varies. It varies on how much you need to use that vocabulary. Skiers have a very extensive vocabulary for snow. English speakers living in Miami probably have a minimal vocabulary for snow, so it depends on the need to use those words. It doesn't mean that English speakers don't perceive of different types of snow, but Eskimo speakers have more of a reason, a need, to use these fine gradations.

We can use this line of reasoning, this vocabulary line of reasoning, to talk about other words as well. In Brazilian Portuguese, for example, there's a word, *saudade*, and it means—it's hard to translate into English—it means a longing, a sort of nostalgia, but it's like a pleasurable feeling tinged with regret or with pain. We don't have a good word for this in English, and not having a good word for it, and it being a very salient and often- used word in Brazilian Portuguese, tells us that there's something going on here. There's something about Brazil and about Brazilians that we can learn because of their emphasis on this word. It doesn't mean that English speakers don't feel the same sort of emotion, but that it is more salient for Portuguese speakers.

Or take the German word *Schadenfreude*; it's the secret delight that one takes in the misfortunes of a friend. Say you have a friend who has a very healthy ego, and some small misfortune—they don't get the raise that they were looking for; they don't get the contract that they were looking for—and you might take a little secret delight in the back of your mind. "I'm glad nothing really bad happened to him, but he needed to be put in his place." Schadenfreude, we've probably all experienced this at one time or another. We don't have a good English word for it; we borrow the German word. It doesn't mean that we don't experience this emotion, but it's not as salient in our own language. There are differences in vocabulary; whether these determine different ways of looking at the world is very much open to question, but they do indicate important differences between cultures.

Whorf's more radical claim concerned grammar. He argued, based on somewhat questionable translations of Hopi, the North American Indian language of Arizona, Whorf argued that they don't have the tense system; they don't have past, present, and future tenses that he assumed to be a sort of natural way of things, or at least the way in which English is organized, so whereas in English we see it is quite natural to say "I saw the girl, I see the girl, I will see the girl," in Hopi those sorts of distinctions aren't made, at least not in the same way. Whorf also argued that the Hopi don't break time up into units the way in which English speakers do. What he used this for, to argue for, and a really neat thing, that the image of a lazy Indian that the Anglos in Arizona and the southwest held about the Hopi was really based on different grammatical structures of verb tenses, and it wasn't that Indians were lazy; they just conceived of time in a different way.

Subsequent research has shown that Whorf actually misunderstood Hopi Indians in fundamental ways. They don't have the same sort of past, present, future tenses that we have in English; instead, they have what are known as validity markers, and so in Hopi, rather than putting a verb tense, you will say whether something is mythic, whether something is known to be true, or whether something is conjectural. These don't make the same distinctions that our verb tenses make in English, but they can get at the same sort of idea. It's a similar kind of categorization. Future events, for example, are always conjectural. Events in the past, which one doesn't know for sure happened, are conjectural as well, so there's a little bit of play there, but more or less you can get the idea of past, present, and future.

Whorf himself observed, "The Hopi language is capable of counting for and correctly describing all observable phenomenon in the universe." Yes, and this has precisely been the critique of Whorf. Yes, Hopi can describe all observable phenomena in the universe; so can every other language. Therefore, how much can language dictate what we think? But that's the critique of Whorf, and I'm going to come back to more critiques in just a moment, but let me give you one more example, and this comes from Yucatec Maya, and I take this example from the worker Victoria Bricker. In Yucatec Maya, there's an obligatory grammatical category called numerical classifiers. This means that every time you mention a number of some object—one, two, three, 500, 1,000, whatever it may be—any time you number an object, you have to use this descriptive classifier with it.

To give you an idea of what these are, at one point there were a couple of hundred of these. Today used in everyday Yucatec speech, there are a couple of dozen, and they're things like elongated, handful of, a chunk of, torn piece, a slice, a slab, a bite. Any time you talk about a plural, or even a singular, if you number an object, you have to use one of these modifiers with it. Therefore, when a

Yucatec speaker talks about three bananas, for example, he or she cannot simply say three bananas, as you would in English. It always has to be modified: three elongated bananas, or three chunks of banana, or three torn pieces of banana. It always has to be modified by one of these numerical classifiers. I would think that Yucatec speakers therefore not only talk about bananas differently, they see them differently. English speakers can see these differences as well, but we don't have to invoke them every time we talk about bananas, but Yucatec speakers do, and so certainly this leads to a different way of perceiving the world.

The linguist Steven Pinker has summarized very effectively a number of arguments against the Sapir-Whorf hypothesis. He notes that first, supposed limitations on expressions in various languages are almost inevitably based on faulty linguistics, such as Whorf's misunderstanding of Hopi. The Hopi do in fact have words for time; the Hopi can in fact talk about time in different ways. Second, that thought is possible without language. We talked about emotions a moment ago, or things that you may see or hear that impact you enough in a non-linguistic or a pre-linguistic way. Babies can think, certainly they can, but they don't have language yet, so thought is possible without language. Finally, language is an inadequate medium for communicating thought. Language always contains ambiguity; what I try and say—I try and be as clear as possible in giving these lectures, for example, but there's always going to be a bit of ambiguity, and what you perceive is going to be different slightly at some points, maybe radically at other points, but it's going to be different than what I intend to say.

While it's difficult to say to what extent language influences thought, there's certainly some sort of relationship here. It's probably not determinate—language doesn't determine thought—but there's a back-and-forth between language and thought, and in this respect it's interesting to look at the recent work done on gender and language. Here I refer particularly to the work of Deborah Tannen, the linguist Deborah Tannen, who's looked at men's speech and women's speech in the United States. She makes a distinction between two types of discourse strategies. One is called rapport, and she associates this more with women, and the other she calls report talk.

In rapport, there's much more of a back-and-forth going on between the two interlocutors, so for example a woman will back-channel (this is a term we use in linguistics) back-channel a lot. When she's conversing with someone, she will give little indicators that she's following along with the arguments and the conversation. It could be nodding the head, it could be saying "Right, uh-huh, yeah," things like this to remain engaged in this back-and-forth of rapport talk, which Tannen associates more with women.

If this doesn't occur, a woman will often use confirmation requests, will ask for her interlocutor to do this, so if somebody's not back-channeling and nodding their head and saying "Right, uh-huh, yeah," then a woman will ask for these by saying, "Right? Huh? What do you think?" or using a final rise in intonation. This is particularly prevalent in teenage girls. "We went to the movies," and it's a statement, it's supposed to be a declarative statement, but it sounds like a question because you rise in intonation. It's asking the person that you're telling the story to, "Give me some help; give me a sign that you're still alive. Nod your head; say yes," and Tannen argues that this is more important for women than it is for men. She argues that men have much more of a direct way of speaking, and this is report talk.

This ties in to another distinction that she makes between men's and women's speech, that women tend to speak more indirectly and men tend to speak more directly. We can see this, and there's a continuum here of directness and indirectness. Tannen says let's take commands, for example. A very direct command would be "Take the garbage out," and then we could move toward more indirect speech: "Take the garbage out, please." "Could you take the garbage out?" "Would you take the garbage out?" Then we can move to the other extreme, a very indirect speech: "The garbage can's full," so not saying what you really want to communicate, "Please take the garbage can out," but just noting this and allowing the other person, "What's today?" "Today's Tuesday." "When does the garbage man come?" something like that, a very indirect way of communicating these ideas.

Tannen also notes that indirect speech includes lots of hedges, and these are qualifications, "I think," "That's what I think," or perhaps things like this to sort of hedge what we're saying, to make it a little bit less direct. She associates this with men's and women's speech, and she's made her career showing how men and women miscommunicate very often in relationships, but it's not that easily divisible. Lots of men have indirect speech patterns. I'm from the south of the United States, and we have more indirect speech than people from the northeast or people from the west, for example. There are lots of women who speak very directly, so we can't correlate this exactly with gender, but there does seem to be some overlap. It also occurs that subordinates tend to talk to their superiors in indirect speech, and superiors talk to their subordinates using direct speech.

This can lead to some problems, and there was research done by a linguist named Charlotte Linde, and she's at the Institute for Research and Learning in Palo Alto, California, and what she's done is analyze the black box recording from airplane crashes. One in particular I'd like to go over today. This occurred on January 13, 1982; it was an Air Florida crash, left from Washington National (today Reagan National), left from Washington National Airport, took off. Just a few seconds after takeoff it crashes into the Potomac. It was in the middle of a winter storm, the Potomac was icy, and 74 out of the 79 people on board died. It turns out later the reason, the cause for the crash, was that ice had formed on the wings. The plane had waited too long after being de-iced. Then it took off, and the rudders and flaps couldn't move, and it crashed into the Potomac.

What Charlotte Linde has done is look at the black box recordings from this flight, and let me read you a little bit of the transcript, and take note of the indirect speech that the copilot is using to communicate his concerns to the pilots.

Copilot: Look at how the hot ice is just hanging there, on this back there. You see that?

Pause. No response. Pause.

Copilot: See all those icicles on the back there and everything?

Captain: Yeah.

Copilot: Boy, this is a losing battle here, trying to de-ice those things. It gives you a false sense of security; that's all it does.

Pause. No response from the pilot. Then they're given clearance for takeoff.

Copilot: Let's check those tops again since we've been sitting here a while.

Captain: I think we're good to go here in a minute.

Copilot: That doesn't seem right, does it? That's not right.

Captain: Yes, it is; there's 80.

Copilot: No, I don't think that's right; maybe it is.

Captain: 120.

Copilot: I don't know.

And then they take off; 37 seconds later, they've crashed, and they haven't communicated anymore. The copilot knew what was going to happen or he suspected what was going to happen, and if he had communicated more directly, rather than using these indirect forms of speech, if he had told the captain, "Hey, I'm not taking off. I'm getting off of this plane because this is dangerous," this could have been averted. It's interesting the way in which indirect speech and direct speech can be used to communicate and miscommunicate with each other.

More sophisticated interpretations of linguistic determinism have recently been produced by scholars such as George Lakoff and Mark Johnson, and they wrote a wonderful little book—it was published in 1980—*Metaphors We Live By*. They argue that there are certain central metaphors in the English language and that these metaphors condition the way in which we think about and thus act in the world. My favorite example that they give is that time is money. In American English they say there's an overarching metaphor that time is money, or that time is a valuable commodity. Based on this overarching metaphor, we create a whole substructure of metaphors: "You're wasting my time." "This gadget's going to save you a lot of time." "How do you spend your time?" "I'm investing a lot of time in doing this project." "I have to budget my time." "Living on borrowed time"—we can go on and on and on.

There are tons of metaphors that tie into this idea that time is a valuable commodity. It's like money: we can spend it, we can save it, we can waste it, we can invest it, and, as a result, we act as if time were a commodity. We use this metaphor as a basis for acting in the world. Another example they give is that argument is war, and again we can give a couple of examples here. You win or lose arguments. Your claims are indefensible, you attack weak points in a person's argument, you can demolish an argument, you can shoot down particular facts, and so forth. We act as if argument is war in some fundamental way. Using such metaphors allows us to invoke powerful presuppositions in our conversation. It allows us these shortcuts when we're communicating with one another because we all understand the metaphorical base of this.

When you presuppose something—this is a very powerful linguistic device—when you presuppose something, you're able to start talking about it like the people that you're talking with know exactly what you're discussing. The most famous example of a presupposition is the joke where a politician is asked, "Have you stopped beating your wife?" That presupposes—I mean, the politician can't—what do you answer? "Yes, I've stopped beating my wife; I used to beat my wife and I've stopped," or you answer "No, no, I haven't stopped beating my wife; I still am." It's very hard to combat that presupposition that's encoded in that first sentence there. Presuppositions are a powerful linguistic tool, but the trick with presuppositions, and this is especially true for me as a lecturer, but for everybody in your everyday conversations the trick is not to presuppose too much or too little.

If I presuppose too much, I could easily right now start talking in the rarefied language of anthropology and social theory, and I could speak over your heads. It doesn't mean that I'm smarter than you; it just means that I command the specialized vocabulary that you haven't studied, so I could presuppose too much and try and wow you now with my knowledge and speak over your head and try and intimidate you in some way. On the other hand, the other danger is presupposing too little and coming off as pedantic, explaining every little thing, and if I did that as a professor you would get bored very quickly. It's the same thing in everyday conversations. We have to figure out what we can presuppose with the person that we're talking with, and we use these as very powerful social tools. A group of your friends, you have little jokes among yourselves; you can presuppose all sorts of knowledge that creates a sense that we are a group and that excludes other people from that group as well, so presuppositions are very powerful political tools to mark social groups, in-group and out-group.

Here, I'd like to briefly review what we've covered so far; we've covered quite a bit of ground today. The Sapir-Whorf hypothesis and its two varieties, strong and weak. The strong version is unprovable; Steven Pinker points out that what we think doesn't always correspond to particular words, as with emotions, for example. He also reminds us of the linguistic fact that every language can communicate any idea that it needs to. The weak version of the Sapir-Whorf hypothesis is much more palatable; certainly language does influence thought, just as thought influences language. It gives us the salient categories with which we can think. You could take Mayan speakers—think about bananas in a particular way. We think about time in a particular way, given our linguistic structures. In the next lecture, we're going to build upon these observations to look at how we construct mental models of how the world operates.

Lecture Eight
Constructing Emotions and Identities

Scope:

In going about our daily lives, we build mental models of the world around us, some highly individual, others more conventional. We are bombarded with so much information in the course of our daily lives that we need the shortcuts provided by mental models (for example, "high price equals high quality") to survive. Mental models, even when they contradict scientific findings, are incredibly resilient, as seen in American folk beliefs about catching a cold from the weather and understanding how a thermostat works.

Often mental models are linguistically based, like scripts that we can enact in greetings and other routinized social settings. But mental models go beyond language to affect us physically. This is best seen in a variety of culturally specific mental illnesses found around the world, from "Arctic hysteria" to the Latin American "evil eye." The anthropologist Nancy Scheper-Hughes has shown how schizophrenia and maternal bonding—seemingly innate phenomena—are differently conceived across cultures. Even something as seemingly natural as gender varies significantly across cultures.

Outline

I. Building on such linguistic research, a new subfield of cognitive anthropology has emerged.

   A. Cognitive models are mental models of how the material and social world works. These may be idiosyncratic or widely shared.

   1. A number of key cognitive models are often set down early in life, through both formal and informal learning.

   2. At the same time, cognitive models are always dynamic and malleable, being formulated and adjusted to meet new circumstances and reconcile new information.

   B. Idiosyncratic (or personal) models develop through one's particular life history.

   1. These include mental prototypes (of a car, dog, or house) and even the definitions of words.

2. Most individuals have idiosyncratic cognitive maps of the areas in which they live.

C. We term cognitive models that are widely shared *cultural models*. Indeed, a useful definition of *culture* is that it is composed of overlapping cognitive models.

  1. Although certain models may be widely shared in a culture, there is never a perfect distribution.

  2. Notions of the American Dream are a cultural model.

II. Cognitive models also affect us physically, in the way that we conceive of illness and the ways we express emotion.

A. There are a number of documented culturally specific diseases, including Arctic hysteria, nervios, and the evil eye. Some of these are psychosomatic, but others are clearly biological ailments.

B. In the United States, for example, we can see the impact of changing cultural notions of illness: the expansion of addiction theories, the explosion of diagnoses for attention deficit syndrome, and the recognition of post-traumatic stress syndrome.

C. Anthropologist Nancy Scheper-Hughes studied schizophrenia in Western Ireland in the mid-1970s. At the time, schizophrenia was associated with post-menopausal women in the United States, but in Ireland, it was almost entirely confined to young celibate men.

  1. Scheper-Hughes worked in the pseudonymous village of Ballybran. The region suffered the effects of massive male migration to larger cities and abroad.

  2. As a result, many households became effectively matrilineal—held together by the mother. Scheper-Hughes argues that such social structure, combined with rigid Catholic teachings on the sinfulness of sexual pleasure, made it difficult for the young men who did not migrate to develop healthy heterosexual relations.

  3. Scheper-Hughes employed Thematic Apperception Tests (TATs) with both schizophrenic and "normal" males. Where the former saw sexual themes, the latter constructed elaborate stories with innocent plots.

    4. Rates of schizophrenia decrease with the distance of migration from one's home village, but rates of alcoholism increase proportionately.

D. Scheper-Hughes went on to conduct ethnographic fieldwork in an impoverished shantytown community in northeastern Brazil, the Alto do Cruzeiro. There, she looked at the way mother-love is expressed.

    1. The Alto do Cruzeiro suffers from extreme poverty and a high infant mortality rate.

    2. Scheper-Hughes showed that mothers in the Alto are very distant with their infants and show little emotion when one dies.

    3. She argues that this is not just an outward stance, but a reflection of the mother's true feelings. She argues that "mother-love" is basically a Western ideology that we have assumed is universal.

III. Just as illnesses and emotions are socially constructed, so, too, is gender, although here, there are more biological constraints.

A. *Sex* refers to the biological categories of male and female. *Gender* refers to the social categories associated with the sexes (femininity and masculinity).

    1. All cultures recognize these two genders, although they assign different meanings to them.

    2. In some cultures, third genders are recognized, such as with the Berdache of the North American Plains Indians.

B. In Samoa, the fa'fa'fine are a recognized third gender.

    1. Fa'fa'fines are boys who choose to dress and act like girls and are raised by their families as girls.

    2. Often misunderstood by Westerners as "gay" or "transvestites," the fa'fa'fines see themselves as fitting in an entirely different category.

C. Research has also shown that the widespread belief in erroneous cultural models can have real-world effects. This is seen in U.S. perceptions of how thermostats function.

Readings:

Nancy Scheper-Hughes, *Saints, Scholars and Schizophrenics.*

———, *Death without Weeping.*

Bradd Shore, *Culture in Mind*.

Questions to Consider:

1. Is mother-love an innate emotion or something learned?

2. Why might different cultures show dramatically different rates of mental illnesses, such as schizophrenia?

3. What are some idiosyncratic mental models you hold? How do these compare to broader cultural models?

Lecture Eight—Transcript
Constructing Emotions and Identities

In the last lecture, we discussed possible ways that language can shape and influence our views of the world, central metaphors for example, but today we're going to turn to cognition and cognitive models. Cognition is the way in which we think; it's the process of thinking; it's the interplay of the mind and how it perceives and interprets the world. Cognitive models then are models of thought, mental models about how the world works, and we're all constantly building up cognitive models, mental models about the world around us and the way in which it works.

In many ways, these are similar to scientific models. We develop hypotheses, we test those, seeing how people in the real world react to our hypotheses, and then we modify those hypotheses. Cognitive models can be more or less idiosyncratic; we can have very particular personal cognitive models about the world around us, or we can have more widely shared or conventional cognitive models, and the more overlapping the cognitive models are between individuals, this is the area that we talk about which is culture. In this lecture, we're going to look at cultural models, cognitive models of illness, of emotions, and of gender, but first I want to begin by talking a little bit about personal cognitive models, idiosyncratic cognitive models, models that are unique to you as an individual based on your own unique life experiences.

Let me start off by doing a sort of psychological experiment. I'll say a word, and picture the first thing that comes into your mind; just note the first image that comes into your mind. Car, what do you imagine when I say car? We probably imagine something fairly similar; it probably has four wheels, it has doors, it has windshields, and so forth, and yet beyond that, the particular sort of car we pictured in our mind's eye probably varies significantly. It could be your car. It could be the car that you would like to have. It might be the car that your parents had when you were a kid. For me, I picture a 1970s Ford LTD or something like a kid would draw, very boxy, four doors, four wheels, and so forth, so we can still talk, we can use the word car, we have this mental prototype of what a car is, but the variation between us is fairly significant as well.

The best example of personal or idiosyncratic mental models is probably maps. What could be more objective than maps, you might think, but we all hold very different mental maps of the world around us. Let's say, if we all lived in the same city we would have very different mental maps of the city. I would know my area of town very well and have a very detailed map, and that detail would probably gradually diminish the farther out I went from my own little section of town. You likewise would have your own areas of town that you would have more detail on, and this would diminish the farther out you went. If we were giving directions to someone how to get from Place A to Place B, you and I would probably use different landmarks. Some would be the same, but we would also have different landmarks and even different routes that we would take. Routes that we would take to work would vary, routes that we would take to the airport.

In the last couple of months, I've taken three trips, taken three taxi rides from my home to the airport, and each time the taxi driver took a different route to the airport. At first, the first time this happened, I was a little bit nervous. I was in the back of the taxi, and I was thinking, Is this guy taking me to some road somewhere out in the middle of nowhere to rob me or kill me. But actually he had thought of a very clever way to go, given rush hour traffic, a route to the airport that I had never thought of it. I took three taxicab rides to the airport in the last month, three different routes, and all different from the normal route that I would take. We have these idiosyncratic models, these mental models, maps of the world, but also maps of the social world, models of the social world.

We also have cultural models, models that are more shared among individuals, broadly shared among members of the same culture, and these shared mental models are really the basis of culture. It's what we talk about when we talk about culture, shared views of looking at the world. A lot of cultural models we use in everyday life are simply handy shortcuts. Take going to buy something, for example. Let's say you're going to buy a bottle of wine. You could spend weeks or months or really even years learning about wine, and you could pick out just the right red to go with that steak. I need a strong Merlot to go with the taste of this steak, or I need a really good Gewurztraminer to offset the spiciness of the hot Thai food we're going to be eating tonight, so we can develop your cognitive models, the cultural models of the wine world.

You could invest the time and develop those very highly, or you could take a shortcut. You could go to the store, and if there's no clerk around to help you, you could say "Well, I want to get a $15 bottle of wine, so I'm going to look through the reds and I'm going to find something in my price range." We use this shortcut, the price, as an indicator of quality. I want to buy a $15 bottle of wine for dinner tonight, or I want to buy a $20 bottle of wine, or I want to buy a $50 bottle of wine, and we're using the shortcut that says that higher price equals higher quality. But, in fact, in lots of blind wine tasting tests, higher price doesn't always equal higher quality. You can get a very good $20 bottle of wine and a very bad $50 or $60 bottle of wine, but we use this as a handy little shortcut. We're bombarded with so much information in our daily lives we have to use these shortcuts to get by. We can't investigate every aspect of every product that we buy, for example, and so we just assume that what's more expensive is better.

That's one example of a cultural model, but let me give you another, a broader or more widely shared notion of a cultural model, and that is of the American Dream. This notion, this Horatio Alger story, if you work hard you'll get ahead and you can move up in the world. We can all pull ourselves up by the bootstraps in the United States. This is a very powerful cultural model for people in the United States and also for other people around the world, particularly immigrants who come to the United States, but look at the facts here.

A recent study showed that 19 percent of Americans believe they are among the top one percent of earners in this country, 19 percent believe they're among the top one percent of earners. Another 20 percent say that one day they will be; one day they're going to be in the top one percent of earners, so 39 percent of Americans think that they're one day going to be among the richest one percent of Americans, and the average median annual income of the richest one percent is $1.5 million a year. It's not going to happen, but having this model, having this cultural model that it's possible, really affects the way in which they feel patriotic, the way in which they feel tied to their country, the way in which they vote, the way in which they act in the world. One point of that is that our cultural models don't have to correspond to material reality. They're just as powerful even if they're not backed up by what's going on in the world around us.

Just as we model the physical world around us in cultural and in idiosyncratic ways, so too we model our own bodies, and here we can talk about body perceptions, the disconnect often between our perceptions of our bodies and the way our bodies actually are. I'm a professor; I work in the universities. There is literally an epidemic these days of eating disorders, particularly among young college-age women, anorexia, bulimia, and very often this results from having a mental image of how their body is that doesn't correspond with what their body actually looks like.

We could also mention powerful cultural models concerning illness, and there are a number of culturally specific illnesses around the world. In Guatemala, where I work, for example, we can talk about one illness called *susto*, or fright, and it's when the soul gets frightened and leaves the body. Let's say you're walking down the road and a snake runs across the road. You could get so frightened that part of your soul leaves your body, and this makes you physically ill. It physically debilitates you; you can lose your appetite, you might become tired, you have a disregard for your personal appearances. It sounds a lot like what we would call depression, clinical depression, but there it's *susto*, and it's treated not by medicines, not by a medical doctor, but by a shaman, who can call the soul back in and reseat it in the body once again.

There are a number of other culturally specific illnesses to the Maya in Guatemala. There's a condition called *nervios*, having nerves. There's a condition of *ojo*, the bad eye; if someone looks at you or looks at one of your children with envy or with greed, again it can steal part of your soul and physically debilitate you, physically make one sick. We would call these psychosomatic illnesses, but for the Maya, with whom I work, these are real illnesses. They are really sick; it's the real deal. This isn't something purely or just only psychological. This is the real cause of their illnesses, and so there are these cultural models of what causes illness surround the world.

Let me just mention a couple of others. The Inuit have a condition called Arctic hysteria; this is only found among the Inuit. At certain points, they will just go crazy. They'll run out of their igloos, they'll rip their clothes off, they'll roll around in the snow; sometimes they'll jump in the water, and sometimes they'll die. Is it cabin fever? Is it deficiency of a particular vitamin? Perhaps, but it's only found among the Inuit, and the Inuit have developed this cultural model to explain it and to understand it, and to work it into their own cultural system. There are other examples: *windingo psychosis*, we find among the Chippewa and the Ojibwa of the northern Great Lakes region, and this is a paranoid belief that others are turning into cannibals and that one might be turning into a cannibal oneself. There's *koro*, which we find in China, the irrational belief that one's genitals are retreating into one's body.

But the best way to illustrate this notion of cultural models of illness is to look at our own society. Take, for example, addiction in the United States. This is a cultural category which has changed radically over the last 20 years or so. For the better or for the worse, I'm not sure, but we've changed the way in which we perceive addiction. We now see it as a real illness. The fact hasn't changed; an alcoholic, a coke addict, any of these people, the physical reality of it is still the same, but the way in which we talk about addiction now, it's not a moral problem. It's a physical problem. It's an illness; it's a real illness that can be treated by medical doctors. Attention deficit hyperactivity disorder, also, similarly, it's a condition unheard of 20 years ago, and now it's estimated that somewhere between four and 12 percent of school-age children suffer from attention deficit hyperactivity disorder, and there's a large percentage—four percent of all children's prescriptions in the United States these days are for Ritalin to treat this disorder that wasn't recognized 20 years ago.

This isn't to say that these aren't real illnesses; it's not to say that our expansion of what we consider to be addictive, not only alcohol and drugs anymore but also gambling and sex and all of these other things, it's not to say that these aren't real illnesses. It's not to say that attention deficit hyperactivity disorder didn't exist 50 years ago, but it existed in a different way. If we didn't recognize it, if we didn't build up a cultural model to culturally sanction this, then it wasn't real in the same way that it's real today. Identifying them makes them more real in a cultural sense, and we can elaborate these cultural models and how these help us form our relationship with reality. We have these culturally specific illnesses round the world.

I want to go into some more detail about a couple of more culturally specific models, both outlined by one anthropologist. Her name is Nancy Scheper-Hughes; she works at the University of California at Berkeley, a very prominent anthropologist. Nancy Scheper-Hughes, she's working in the mid-1970s in Western Ireland. She goes to this small village in Western Ireland which she uses a pseudonym for, she calls Ballybran, and what she finds there is what we would consider to be a particularly dysfunctional system, dysfunctional in all sorts of ways. It's a very poor part of Ireland. There's a lot of out migration. Males are leaving their home villages and going to work in London or immigrating to the States, leaving their home villages. Children, particularly the sons, are also leaving; the older sons leave and the younger sons are left behind, so as a result you have families that are really matriarchal in many ways. You have a woman and her children. The older sons as they get older will leave, and the daughters and the younger children will stay at home.

This creates this virtual matriarchy in Northern Ireland and Western Ireland, and as a result there's a very tight bond between brothers and sisters, the brothers that stay behind, the younger brothers that stay behind, and their sisters, and Nancy Scheper-Hughes argues, and quite controversially, I will add, that the combination of the Catholic doctrine about sex that's practiced in this part of Western Ireland, that sex is a dirty thing, it's a nasty thing, it's something that's only for reproduction, it's something that we really shouldn't talk about, and this is an area of Ireland where they have a really strict Catholicism, combine this view of sex with the demographic fact that most of the males are migrating out, and you have these households being run by women, a few males in the household, but as a result of these two factors, the youngest boys who stay behind have a really hard time overcoming their Oedipal complex, incestuous feelings toward their mother and toward their sisters.

She also finds, and these are quite remarkable figures here, she finds, and this was a survey that she did in 1971, that 20 percent of the men in Western Ireland at this time were in a mental hospital, 20 percent of the male population were in a mental hospital. Remember, this is mostly the younger children, the younger male children that stayed behind; the others have migrated out. Of those, 89 percent were celibate—89 percent had never had sex—and half were diagnosed with schizophrenia, so you have 20 percent of the men in a mental institution: 89 percent of those are celibate and half of those are diagnosed with schizophrenia. At the time—this has changed a bit in the States since then—but at the time, schizophrenia in the United States was associated with middle-aged married women, very much a middle-aged married woman's disease, but in Ireland it was these bachelor men, the celibate bachelor men, and why is this?

Scheper-Hughes said it's because they have a hard time overcoming, handling their sexuality, overcoming their heritage and handling their sexuality in a productive way. They've been raised in this household, in a society that's ostensibly patriarchal, led by a man, but in this case the elder men have left and it's run by a woman, and so they never really overcome their psychosexual feelings toward their mothers and toward their sisters either, and it's very hard for them to establish a healthy relationship with other women. As a sideline here, it's interesting to note that with the distance of migration away from Western Ireland, the rates of schizophrenia went down. The farther men left, the farther away they went when they left, the lower the rates of schizophrenia, but there was a proportional increase in the rates of alcoholism the farther away men left.

I'm trying to tie this into cultural models, and to do this, one of the techniques that Nancy Scheper-Hughes used was to show her subjects TATs, Thematic Apperception Tests. It's a test used by psychologists; it's sort of like a Rorschach test, except it's a real image. They're charcoal drawings, and you can see real people—it's not abstract—so you show these images to a person and ask them to describe what's going on in the picture. In one picture in particular, there was an image of a woman, a bare-breasted woman, lying in bed with the covers pulled up to right underneath her breasts, and a man standing beside the bed, turning away, sort of with his arm over his face a little bit, as if he were ashamed just a bit.

She shows this to the men in Ballybran, this town in which she's working, and asks them to describe what was going on. Healthy men, the normal men, the non-schizophrenic men that she interviewed, would give stories such as, "There was a boating accident, and his sister fell into the water, and her clothes were wet, and so he's brought her back home and undressed her and put her into bed, and now he's turning away." The schizophrenic man would say,

"They've just had sex, and now the man is embarrassed. He's feeling bad about this; he's feeling guilty, and that's the reason that he's turning way." Some very different interpretations of the same images, and I'll mention here that when I show these images to my undergraduate students, sex is inevitably one of the primary themes. Either I'm dealing with a lot of schizophrenics or what we consider to be schizophrenia varies dramatically from culture to culture.

Nancy Scheper-Hughes went on to write her next big book, another very important work in anthropology, about Brazil, where she had worked earlier in the 1960s as a Peace Corps volunteer before she went to graduate school. She goes back to northeastern Brazil after she's worked in Ireland, a little town that she calls, using a pseudonym, Bom Jesus, and really she worked in the shantytown on the edge of this Brazilian city, and the shantytown was called Alto do Cruzeiro. This is a big sugar cane region; the Amazon jungle in this area has been cut down. If you look at satellite photographs, the National Geographic satellite photographs, this is the splotch of brown in the middle of all of this Amazon region because it's all been cut down to grow sugar cane.

It's an extremely poor part of Brazil, poverty in the way they can we can hardly even imagine, poverty of people going hungry, dying of hunger, literally dying of hunger, and experiencing the delirium that goes with dying of hunger and when your body starts eating itself from the inside out. You may have gone hungry for a day, or you may have felt hungry one day, but it's hard for us to relate with this kind of hunger. We've never felt this kind of hunger, not eating for days at a time. In the Alto do Cruzeiro, in the shantytown on the edges of this Brazilian city, most of the people work in sugar plantations. Some of the women work as domestic help.

It's very harsh conditions. There's a very high death rate, poverty and hunger are extremely high, and the infant mortality rate is astronomical. The average woman in this community has 9.5 pregnancies in her lifetime and 3.5 child deaths, so the average woman has 3.5 of her children die. Most of these occur before six months of age and virtually all of them before one year old. In addition, they have an average of 1.5 stillbirths, so the average woman in the shantytown, the Alto do Cruzeiro in Brazil, the average woman gets pregnant 9.5 times, and a total of five of those, over half, results in the death of the baby, either through a stillbirth or through an infant death. Nancy-Scheper Hughes sees this, and she notices that the women aren't mourning over their dead infants. They go to the grave, they bury their babies, but they don't cry, and in fact she titled her book on the subject *Death Without Weeping*.

She asked herself: What's going on here? Why are these mothers not crying when their babies die? She says we have this idea in the West that we consider to be totally natural, that women bond with their children. It's like a woman gives birth, and we expect the violins to go up in the background and this instant bonding. The baby is put in the mother's arms and there's this instant metaphysical bonding between mothers and their children, this moment of epiphany, and, in fact, and there's been some recent research done on this showing that a lot of post-birth depression results from women not experiencing this instant bonding, and that all women don't experience this feeling, and a lot of women feel guilty if they don't because we've built it up to be such a romantic ideal in our culture that everybody needs to experience this same sort of bonding, that it's supposed to be natural; it's the natural scheme of things.

But here, the women don't cry when their babies die, and why is that? Nancy Scheper-Hughes says, because the conditions are so harsh, they don't want to put any emotional attachment into these children until they're over a year old, until they know that they're going to survive and that they're going to live and this relationship can really flourish. And so what Nancy Scheper-Hughes argues is that this notion of mother-love is really, in her words, a bourgeois myth. It's a myth developed in the West that romanticizes a natural bond between mothers and their children that doesn't have to exist, that doesn't exist in this area of northeastern Brazil, where the women don't cry when their children die.

This research has created quite a stir in the academy. A lot of people think that there is a natural bond. Sociobiologists, for example, would argue that we have evolved an evolutionary propensity for women to become attached to their children, and Nancy Scheper-Hughes says no, this is a cultural model. It's a cultural model that's especially insidious because we take it to be the natural scheme of things. But, she says, in Alto do Cruzeiro, where they have these lifeboat ethics, where you know people are going to die, the chances are greater than 50 percent that any child a woman has is going to die, why invest all that time and attention in that child? We have these cultural models of illness around the world, sometimes radically different models about the relationship between mothers and children and the nature of mother-love.

I would also like to mention in the lecture today about cultural models of another thing we take to be quite natural, which is gender. Of course, there are women and men in the world. Men act one way, women act another, and this is just the natural scheme of things. But, in fact, there's quite a bit of variation in the way in which men and women are expected to act in different cultures. Every culture around the world recognizes two genders, a masculine gender and a feminine gender, and here let me make a distinction. We use gender to refer to the social categories associated with masculinity and femininity, and we use sex more precisely to describe biologically male and females.

Every culture around the world recognizes at least two genders, but some cultures recognize a third gender. Take, for example, the berdache, these so-called two-spirit people of the Pueblo Indians, the Zuni and the Navajo. These were men, biologically men, but they lived as women. They dressed as women did, they did women's work, and it turns out that they were very highly valued because women were seen as potentially polluting, and so on hunting trips and in important rituals shamans didn't want to take women along because they could corrupt the hunt because they're just a little bit polluting, so they could take along these berdache, these men-women who could do all of the cooking, who could do all of the taking care of the clothes and so forth on the hunting trips, and yet wouldn't corrupt the nature of the hunt or this contact with the spirit world in certain rituals.

On Samoa, remember Samoa, where Margaret Mead studied and romanticized the sexual life of the people of Samoa, on Samoa there's a group of people call fa'fa'fines. *Fa'fa'fine* means in the manner of a woman, and these fa'fa'fine, they are males who wear women's dress, who do women's work, and they're fairly highly valued among Samoan families because they can do both things that men can do and things that women can do. But these fa'fa'fines, when you talk to them, they say that they're really uncomfortable with foreigners who try and categorize them in a specific way. If they go, if these Samoan fa'fa'fines, when they go to Australia on vacation, they say, "All the Australians think that we're transvestites or we're gays, and we're not. We're a different sort of thing. We're a third gender; we're neither male nor female. We don't fit into this Western binary opposition."

These are some pretty radical differences: mother-love, conceptions of mother-love in different cultures; conceptions of gender in different cultures. And I would like to end here on somewhat of a lighter note, another example of cultural models, and one that comes from our own culture. Let me ask you something. Let's say that it's extremely cold outside and you go back to your home and the heat has been turned off, and you go inside and it's freezing cold. You've just been out in the cold, and you really want to get your house warmed up quickly. What do you do? You go over to the thermostat, and let's say that your ideal temperature would be 78°. What do you set the thermostat on? Lots of people that I ask this question to in my classes, and lots of people in the States as a whole, would say "I would go in, and first I would turn it up to 90° and get it really nice and warm, and then I would go back and turn it to 78°."

This is a very particular cultural model of the way in which a thermostat and heating works. It's a valve model; we're picturing the thermostat like the valve on a faucet that we can open it up wider and more hot air will come out. In fact, the way in which heating works, it's this binary operation. The heating elements either come on or they turn off, and it's not this gradation. The air isn't hotter or colder. The fan can blow; you can put the fan on low or you can put the fan on high, so the fan can blow at different speeds, but actually the operation of the heating system is binary, off or on. Having a cultural model, though, that it's like a valve, has real-world implications. If we go in, the house is freezing cold, we turn the thermostat on 90° and then we forget it. We go out and we run an errand or something, we come back and the house is burning up, and we've wasted all of this electricity that we didn't need to do because if you had set the thermostat on 78° in the first place it would have gotten to that temperature just as quickly as if you had set it on 90°.

Mental models are the way in which we look at the world; these can be more or less idiosyncratic. The less idiosyncratic or the more conventional they are, this is what creates what we call culture. Today we looked at cultural models of disease, of emotion, of mother-love, of gender, and to the ways in which cultural models can influence our own behavior: when we go shopping, equating high price with quality, for example, or the way in which we use thermostats in our homes or apartments. In the next lecture, what we're going to do is apply the scheme of cultural models to the Fulbe of northern Cameroon.

Lecture Nine
Magic, Religion, and Codes of Conduct

Scope:

Anthropologists, when discussing spirituality (a belief in souls), often distinguish between *magic* and *religion*. Magical beliefs hold that humans can control natural and supernatural forces; that is, magical rites, if conducted properly, should have a desired practical result (such as making the rain come). Religion, in contrast, rests on the belief that humans are subjects of a higher power; rather than controlling the spiritual world, they must do its bidding and seek their desires through prayer and supplication. In practice, the distinction between religion and magic often breaks down.

In this lecture, we look to the Fulbe of northern Cameroon, a nominally Muslim culture with a rich tradition of magical beliefs. The Fulbe world is inhabited by cannibal witches, but it is the Islamic Mullam who has the power to cure their soul-eating illness. We see also how women are treated in this patriarchal system and the unexpected ways in which they are able to assert their power.

Outline

I. All cultures have spiritual beliefs, although these vary greatly from society to society.

   A. Edward Tylor, in his 1871 book *Primitive Cultures*, observed that a belief in souls ("animism") is found in all cultures.

   B. The distinction between magic and religion goes back to another early anthropologist, James Frazer, who wrote an encyclopedic survey of the world's religions in *The Golden Bough* (1922).

      1. In his formulation, magic is directed toward immediate problems. It seeks to force supernatural powers to do one's will in a sort of "primitive science."

      2. Accusations of sorcery and witchcraft serve important social functions.

   C. Religion is conceived as more conciliatory toward the supernatural, involving prayer and supplication to a higher power. Religion is usually highly organized and revolves around group activities.

II. The Fulbe of Domaayo in northern Cameroon illustrate how difficult it often is to distinguish between magic and religion.

    A. The Fulbe are an ethnic group that lives across West Africa.

        1. There are some 8 to 10 million Fulbe peoples, who are also known as the Fulani. They all speak varieties of the language Fulfulde.

        2. The Fulbe are mostly Muslim, and they trace their origins to the *jihads* that expanded Islam to this part of Africa in the early 19th century.

        3. The Fulbe have a chiefdom system of traditional organization, but today, they all live under modern nation-states.

    B. Domaayo is a small Fulbe town in northern Cameroon that has been studied by anthropologist Helen Regis.

        1. Cameroon—first a German, then a French colony—gained its independence in 1960.

        2. Domaayo (population about 1,000) is located far to the north, far from the capital and much of the country's political and economic life.

    C. *Pulaaku* is the Fulbe code of conduct. It mandates stoicism, the withholding of emotion, and a clear deference to elders.

    D. The Fulbe are farmers, but they see themselves more as cattle herders.

        1. Farmers mostly grow millet, which, served as porridge, is the staple of the local diet.

        2. But the Fulbe were historically cattle herders—and most still are although not in Domaayo. Fulbe culture tends to equate farmers with pagans because most farmers they come into contact with are not Muslim.

        3. Thus, for the Fulbe, the difference between farmers and herders is an important symbolic distinction, and given that they are not pagans, they must be herders.

        4. This provides evidence for Claude Lévi-Strauss's idea that humans tend to organize the world through binary oppositions, the most crucial of which is culture and nature.

E. The Fulbe are a patrilineal society.

    1. Men may have more than one wife, but all wives have to be cared for in good fashion. Men are required to supply their wives with annual gifts of cloth.

    2. Women are seen as potentially dangerous, and there is a fairly rigid segregation of the sexes. Men do not interact much with their wives.

    3. Divorce is not uncommon and may be initiated by either the husband or the wife. The average woman will be married 2.6 times in her lifetime.

III. Although Fulbe society is nominally Muslim, its members also maintain a dynamic indigenous tradition of magical beliefs.

    A. Virtually everyone in Domaayo self-identifies as Muslim, although some are recognized as being more pious than others.

        1. *Mallum* is a term of respect bestowed upon a man who has read the whole Koran. Mallums serve as Koranic teachers and village elders. They also play important roles in native religious rituals and beliefs.

        2. Boys and girls are expected to attend Koranic schools, where they learn to read and write and memorize scripture. Girls, however, drop out by the time they are 12 or 13, while boys continue with their studies.

        3. It is too easy to lump together all of the Muslim world into a single culture area. The Fulbe practice just one of countless varieties of Islam practiced around the world.

        4. Indeed, the Fulbe are generally devout, especially in following the customs of daily prayers and celebrating holy days.

    B. The Fulbe do not restrict their spiritual beliefs to Islamic traditions. They also see the world as inhabited by malevolent spirits that must be averted with magic. Children are especially vulnerable to spiritual illnesses.

        1. Looking at a child with an envious eye can actually cause deadly physical illness for the child. Therefore, adults treat their children with what seems to foreigners as a distant nonchalance.

2. Children are also given protective amulets to wear; these may contain magical talismans and written verses from the Koran.

3. A pregnant woman should avoid looking at a lizard or her child might have a wasting disease. If a pregnant woman looks at an antelope, however, the child may take on the long, graceful features that the Fulbe see as an ideal of beauty.

C. The scariest creature in the Fulbe pantheon of demons is the cannibal witch.

1. Cannibal witches eat the intestines and souls of their victims, who in turn, become cannibal witches.

2. The Fulbe prize meat, which they feel they do not get enough of. It is also said that human flesh is the best in the world. Thus, the image of the cannibal witch, while it is feared, is also understood.

3. Too much desire (which goes against the code of *pulaaku*) is dangerous. The desire for meat brings one dangerously close to being a cannibal witch.

D. Women have a wide range of their own medicinal magic, including birth-control potions. They are especially vulnerable to the river spirits, because they often go alone to fetch water. Attacks from river spirits must be treated by a Mallum, or a woman could die.

Readings:

Helen Regis, *The Fulbe of Northern Cameroon*.

Claude Lévi-Strauss, *The Raw and the Cooked*.

Questions to Consider:

1. What social functions do witchcraft beliefs and accusations serve in other cultures?

2. How do the Fulbe reconcile their Muslim faith with their magic practices?

3. How do stories of river spirits convey Fulbe perceptions of white people?

Lecture Nine—Transcript
Magic, Religion, and Codes of Conduct

In the last lecture, we talked about cognitive models, mental models of how the world works, and really this is in many ways our reality, the reality that we live in. These models may be highly idiosyncratic, our personal quirks, the uniqueness of our personality, or they can be more widely shared: the proper distance to stand from someone; what to do when the national anthem plays, and so forth, and to the extent to which these are shared, they constitute what we call culture. In this lecture, what I would like to do is apply our understanding of cultural models to a particular case, and that is the Fulbe of northern Cameroon, and, in particular, I'm going to talk about three aspects of Fulbe culture. The first is their code of conduct, which is called *pulaaku*. The second is their self-identity as Muslim herders, even though they're farmers. Third is the relationship between religion and magic. They're an Islamic culture although they still have a rich tradition of indigenous magical beliefs.

There's been a long concern in anthropology with religion and magic and with various forms of spirituality. Edward Tylor, the man who gave us that classic definition of culture, noted that every culture around the world has a conception of some sort of soul, of some sort of spirituality. He believed that in primitive culture, the belief in the soul emerged from dreams, from trying to come up with an explanation for dreams. It seemed to these people that a part of their body had to leave and go somewhere else, and so they assumed that there was a part of their body which wasn't physical, a soul. Tylor argued that this belief in souls eventually evolved—he called it animism, a belief in souls—and that this eventually evolved into polytheism and finally into monotheism, which he took as a hallmark of civilization. Tylor gave us the idea of animism, a belief in souls, and this is found in all cultures around the world. Our own culture generally conceives of souls as being uniquely human, but in many cultures souls can be found in animals, in plants, in rocks, and the inanimate world as well.

We have Tylor. Another important early scholar on the anthropology of religion was James Frazer, and in 1922 he published a book, *The Golden Bough*. At first, it was a two-volume series, and he expanded it over the years into 13 volumes. It was an encyclopedic coverage of religious practices around the world, and it's a classic text in anthropology and in religious studies to this day. In this book, Frazer made a crucial distinction that we still hold today between magic and religion, and he argued that magic is a type of primitive science. It's a belief that we can control the world around us, the spiritual world, the supernatural world, and that if we do certain rituals, if you do certain rituals, just like in a scientific experiment, if you follow the plan exactly, a predetermined outcome will occur. If we follow all of the rules of the rain dance ritual, for example, and we don't bring along any menstruating women, if we don't have sex for a week before we conduct the ritual and we do the rain dance properly, the rain has to come. It's a belief that humans can control the supernatural world and their natural environment.

That's magic, and he contrasted this with religion, and religion sees humans as being more at the mercy of a higher power. This is a sort of spirituality associated with a conciliatory view toward a higher power, a larger power, recognizing that we're at the mercy of something greater than ourselves. In Frazer's scheme, prayer is crucial to religion because prayer is requesting something from a supernatural being. It's not demanding something, it's not making something happen, but it's supplicating, asking for a favor from the greater powers that be. Now religion generally is also more highly organized, more large-scale, often has a written tradition to distinguish it from magic.

Taking this into account, the difference between religion and magic, I would like to turn now to the Fulbe of northern Cameroon. The Fulbe, they're an ethnic group. There are about 8 to 10 million Fulbe living in western Africa, and they range all the way from Senegal, far in the west, all the way over to Chad, Sudan, and Cameroon. They speak varieties of the Fulbe language. Most of them are cattle herders, which is a very common economic pattern in western Africa. Most of them are Muslims; they trace their history back to jihads in the 19th century, which was moving Islam westward. They were traditionally organized into chiefdoms, although today all Fulbe live within the boundaries of modern nation-states.

The anthropologist Helen Regis has worked among the Fulbe in a community in northern Cameroon, a community that she calls

Domaayo. This is a pseudonym, but it's a community in northern Cameroon, a small village of about 1,000 people. There's a little mosque, a small government health center, a local school, but in many respects Domaayo is far removed from national Cameroonian life. National life in Cameroon is oriented around the port cities and the capital, and Domaayo way to the north is far removed from the workings of national life.

Ostensibly, Domaayo is ruled by the laws of Cameroon, but actually, in fact, in daily life it's governed more by a moral code called pulaaku. Pulaaku is a moral code that really stresses stoicism. One should always refrain from displaying emotions; one shouldn't show anger or grief or love. Even physical pain should be endured silently. In terms of this moral code, pulaaku, men are especially expected to adhere to it closely, and there's even some competition between men of who can embody the most pulaaku. For example, the staple diet among the Fulbe is millet porridge, and they'll serve this in a bowl along with a little sauce for spice. They'll serve this in a common bowl, and everybody will dip out of it with their hands and eat from their hand. If a man dips into a scalding hot bowl of millet porridge, he's not supposed to show any pain or any emotion and take it up, put it into his mouth and eat it like nothing has happened, and then pass it on to the next unsuspecting man sitting next to him.

Women also are expected to adhere to pulaaku, although they're given a little bit more leeway. Under the rules of pulaaku, anger should always be muted, grief should always be muted, no powerful emotion should be shown. Regis writes about child deaths, the number of child deaths that have occurred in Domaayo while she's been there, and this is a fairly poor region of West Africa and so child deaths are not unheard of. She notes that the women in Domaayo, when their children die, refrain from crying at their child's death. You'll recall Nancy Scheper-Hughes, working in the northeast of Brazil, also noted that poor Brazilian women didn't cry when their children died. *Death Without Weeping* was the name of the Nancy Scheper-Hughes book.

In contrast to Scheper-Hughes, Regis argues that the women in Domaayo do feel grief when their children die, but it's muted. It's muted because it's filtered through this cultural model of pulaaku. Being too much in love with one's wife is similarly seen as being a bad thing, a violation of pulaaku; it's akin to a mental illness because there's a passion there, a passion that one expresses, a passion that can be debilitating to the individual. Excessive laughter, happiness, all of these emotions have to be muted under the code of pulaaku. It doesn't mean that the Fulbe don't experience happiness, that they don't experience love or grief or pain or any of these emotions; they just express it in a very different way.

Now pulaaku is also closely tied to notions of respect and modesty. One should always have respect for elders in this society, and yet one can never be too modest, the Fulbe say. And so in pulaaku, we have this cultural concept, this cultural model, tied to relations of respect and modesty, and it's a cultural model that people talk about openly. Many cultural models, perhaps most cultural models, are less implicit in cultures. They go without saying and they come without saying. But the pulaaku moral code is debated very often among the Fulbe trying to figure out exactly where to draw these lines about what is acceptable behavior and what isn't.

One thing about cultural models is they don't have to conform to what we would consider to be the objective reality, the objective world, truth. Take cultural models that we mentioned last time of the thermostat. Many people in the country hold a valve model of how a thermostat works. This isn't objectively true, it's not scientifically true, and yet it is their reality, and they act on that reality, so it becomes real in some meaningful way. We as human beings, with these huge brains that we've been given by evolution, we have an incredible capacity for cognitive dissonance, holding contradictory beliefs at the same time. For example, let's take the Fulbe and their image of themselves as compared to reality.

The Fulbe of Domaayo are farmers. They raise millet; you'll remember that millet porridge is the staple of the Fulbe diet, millet porridge mixed with a little bit of sauce. Millet in many ways is at the heart of the Fulbe economy and at the heart of the Fulbe symbolic life. But these Fulbe don't see themselves as farmers; they see themselves as herders, as cattle herders. Most of the other Fulbe people in western Africa are cattle herders, and they come from this tradition of being cattle herders, so even though the villagers of Domaayo are farmers themselves, they don't like to be associated with farmers. This doesn't mean that they're delusional; they do have some cattle. They wouldn't say that we don't farm at all, but their self-image of themselves as a group is of being Muslim herders.

They contrast this with their neighbors, their pagan neighbors whom they call the Mundang, and they view the Mundang as being almost subhuman. They're not Muslim, so they're pagan; they're farmers, and the Fulbe of Domaayo want to distance themselves as much as possible from the Mundang. We're Muslim, we're civilized, we're the real people, and these Mundang are pagan farmers. They don't believe in the teachings of Islam, they're not like us, they're subhuman, they're more of nature than of culture, so this interesting disconnect between the Fulbe cultural model of themselves and the reality of their subsistence points to the fluidity of identity.

What does it mean to be Fulbe? In a sense, it means to be a cattle herder because most Fulbe are cattle herders, and this is the origin of Fulbe culture; yet the Domaayo have found themselves in a situation where they have to be or they want to be farmers and yet still consider themselves to be Fulbe, so they have this paradoxical association between herding and farming. This brings to mind a distinction made by the famous French anthropologist Claude Levi-Strauss, and he says that human beings tend to think in dichotomies, that mental models ultimately boil down to binary oppositions. For the Fulbe, they consider themselves to be real humans in contrast to the Mundang, who they consider to be pagans and almost subhumans, so this idea of us against them, the believers against the pagans, the herders versus the farmers, the Fulbe and the Mundang.

Levi-Strauss's most impressive work is a series of books that he published starting in the mid-1960s up through the early 1970s called *Mythologiques*, and the first was *The Raw and the Cooked*, the second was *From Honey to Ashes*, the third was *On the Origin of Table Manners*, and the fourth was *The Naked Man*. What Levi-Strauss did in the series of books was he took 813 myths, and he started with the Bororo, who live in the Amazonian rain forest, and he moved up through each of these books up through South America, up through Central America, all the way up the northwest coast of North America up to the Inuit speakers, and he traced their mythologies and he said that all of the mythologies of both continents, this whole hemisphere, boil down to one basic dichotomy, a dichotomy that can be extrapolated out to other realms, and that dichotomy is the distinction between nature and culture.

He says that it's almost human nature to distinguish between nature and culture. Nature is chaotic, it's unruly, and culture is ordered and civilized, so we have nature is to culture as chaos is to order, as pagans are to believers, for example. Culture is civilization; it's who we are. We can control what we do within our culture; outside of our culture area, in the wilds of nature, we cannot control the forces that go on there, so nature is to culture as chaos is to order. It's also, as Levi-Strauss pointed out, as raw is to cooked. Raw food starts out in nature, it's picked, it's brought into the cultural realm physically by cooking it, and it becomes a cultured product. Cooked food is more cultured; we take it out of nature and we make it culture. That was the myth that he started out with among the Beroro, that raw concerned the origin of cooking food.

He moves up through these four volumes and these 813 myths up to the Inuit, and he finds the central metaphor, the central dichotomy in Inuit mythology, is naked and clothed. They're living way up north. I mean, clothing is obviously very important to us, but clothing is also something that makes us human, that sets us off from nature. We wear clothes, we have some sense of modesty, so we're not the animals of nature. Nature is to culture as animal is to human, and Levi-Strauss went on to argue as women are to men. In many cultures around the world, women are considered to be more natural, more chaotic, not as civilized as men.

There's this notion that women are a little more dangerous because they're more in touch with this natural side of things, and we see this among the Fulbe. Fulbe men, it's a nominally patriarchal society but Fulbe men have a real fear of women, so perhaps there's something to Levi-Strauss's idea, some sort of binary basis in our minds for these kinds of cultural models. Or perhaps we could take an analogy from quantum physics. Rather than saying that things are binary in quantum physics, what we've traditionally seen as being binary, either off or on, one or zero, they can be both at the same time, off and on, one and zero, just as the Fulbe can simultaneously be farmers and herders in a meaningful way.

Men and women in Fulbe society, Fulbe women go and live with their husbands' families, and as a result they're always outsiders.

They leave their own family, and they go and live with their husband's family. If their husband dies, if they get divorced, they have to depend on their children to help care for them because they have left their natal family behind when they get married. Fulbe society tends towards patriarchy, or male dominance. The male ideology is patriarchal; they want to keep women subordinated, keep them in their place. It's not extreme, but they're definitely patriarchal. Fulbe men may have more than one wife, but a man has to care for each of his wives in a proper fashion, a fashion fitting their rank in society. If they don't care for their wives, that's grounds for divorce, and divorce is not unheard of. This is an Islamic society, but nonetheless women can initiate divorce, and in fact the average Fulbe woman has over two husbands, over 2.5 husbands in her lifetime.

When they get married, men have to compensate their wife's family. They're taking her away, they're taking this reproductive resource away from the wife's family and bringing it into their family, so they have to pay, and what they pay is what we call in anthropology bride price, the price that a husband pays for his wife. In Fulbe society, this payment occurs through cloth. Fulbe women use bolts of cloth— they're about 6 yards long—that they use to make skirts and blouses from, so this cloth is very important in Fulbe society. The best cloths, a man who pays a high price for his wife will give wax cloths, and these are made using a batik method, where wax is put onto the cloth and then it's dyed and it comes out with these incredibly intricate patterns; so the best cloths are these wax cloths, and they're generally imported—they're not made locally. They come from Nigeria, but more often from Java and from the Netherlands, so a powerful man, a man who wants to keep his status in society, who wants to marry a good woman, a good woman from a good lineage, will have to supply lots of these wax cloths to her and to her family in order to secure her hand in marriage.

Less desirable are print cloths that are made to mimic the look of wax cloths, and these are made in Cameroon and other African countries, and today, actually, a great number of them are made in Asia, so if a man doesn't have a lot of money, he doesn't have a lot of resources, he can't pay a high bride price, then he will give these print cloths. There's always this economic component to the negotiation of marriage. The woman's family is trying to get the best payment they can for the woman; the man is trying to give as little as he can, and this occurs not only at the moment of marriage but throughout their marriage, throughout their time together. Every year, the man has to give his wife gifts of cloth, preferably wax cloth, but in a rough situation he can give print cloths as well.

And so men see the women as dangerous, and, as a result, there's a strict segregation of the sexes in Fulbe society. A man has to get married; it's seen as an imperative of a Fulbe man. He can't make his own millet; that would be humiliating. A man has to have a wife at home who can care for his children and do all of the things that a man has to have done for him. But men don't interact with their wives very much, and they prefer that their wives not go out in the street very often, either, so there's a segregation between the sexes, partly due to the fact that women are seen as polluting, and if men have too much contact with women, then they can get polluted as well and get debilitated.

Fulbe is a Muslim culture, at least nominally a Muslim culture. Virtually everyone in the town of Domaayo is Muslim, and they're devout Muslims in their own way. There are local Koranic teachers called Mallums, and a Mallum is a person who has read the whole Koran from front to back, and these are spiritual guides in Domaayo society. They also serve as magical healers, something we'll come back to in just a moment. Girls normally go to the Koranic school as well as boys. The girls will only go until about age 12 or 14, at which point they get married and they drop out school. The boys will continue on with their Koranic education.

Let me make a point here about Islam, it's misleading to talk about Islam as if it were a unified, singular, monolithic religion. It's impossible to say that Christians believe X. We have such a wide variety of Christianity: the Greek Orthodox church, the Roman Catholic church, the Church of God, the Church of Christ, Methodist, Episcopalians, it goes on and on, so think of all of these varieties of Christianity. It's hard to say what Christians believe, and the same holds true of Islam. Islam is also a religion of great diversity, and the Islam of these Mallums of Domaayo is very far removed from the Islam of Osama bin Laden or the Taliban in Afghanistan, for example. The Fulbe, like people across Africa, like people across the Middle East and central Asia as well, have adopted

Islam, but it's combined, it's fundamentally mixed and melded with traditional religious practices, what Frazer would have called magic. The people of Domaayo are very devout Muslims. On the one hand, they practice daily prayers, they fast during Ramadan, and they see no contradiction in doing all of this and at the same time using amulets, for example, to protect their children against spirits and demons and souls that live in the Fulbe area.

The Fulbe world is inhabited by these spirits that are potentially detrimental, and the Fulbe believe that children are especially vulnerable to spirit attack, and the younger they are, the more susceptible they are to attack by spirits and demons. They believe, the Fulbe believe that it's very dangerous to be too loving toward a child, and as a result Fulbe mothers and Fulbe fathers, Fulbe adults, take what we would consider to be a very nonchalant attitude, if not negligent attitude, toward their children. They don't run over immediately when they're crying to cuddle them and kiss them and make them feel better. They don't do a lot of things that we would consider to be natural signs of loving a child because they believe if you lavish too much attention on a child it's going to hurt that child, it's going to steal part of their spirit, and others who pay too much attention to your children are hurting that child as well.

If a neighbor woman looks at your child very lovingly, it's really a love of envy there and a love of greed, and that greed can physically hurt the child and result in physical debilitation, so one of the worst things that you can do in Fulbe society is what would seem quite natural to an American. If you walked into a Fulbe household and you saw a child, and you went over and patted its head and pinched its cheek and said, "This is just the cutest kid I've ever seen in my life," this would be an awful insult and an awful danger to the child by paying too much attention to it. What the parents do to protect their children is they put amulets around their necks, and it's interesting here that the most powerful amulets are those that contain passages of the Koran, written down on a piece of paper, rolled up and then put into the amulet, and the word of the Koran has special preventative powers in keeping these souls from being stolen. And here we see a mix of what Frazer would have called magic and religion—Islam, certainly a religion; these beliefs about demons and spirits, certainly magic—so we see this intimate mixing of these two sorts of beliefs.

Women are important medical practitioners in Fulbe society. Women keep a little medicine chest—a lot of this involves fertility. Often in the medicine chest there will be a bit of an umbilical cord from a child, and if a woman is infertile they will conduct rituals with this umbilical cord to make her fertile once again. Women also control a body of knowledge concerning herbal potions that can be used as birth control, for example, or day-after potions, if you will, so women serve this important medical function, this religious medical function in Fulbe society.

In terms of spiritually caused illnesses, the worst fate that can befall a Fulbe person is an attack by a cannibal witch. The cannibal witches come and they eat one's insides. They eat one's intestines, and they also steal part of one's soul. In stories about this, they tell of a bird that will fly out of the anus of a cannibal witch, and it carries a torch of fire with it, and it goes and attacks people, steals their intestines, steals part of their soul, and goes back and takes it to the cannibal witch, who can pig out on this human flesh. Why is this such a fear for Fulbe people? Let's remember that the Fulbe of Domaayo are farmers, but they see themselves as herders. They used to be part of this herding tradition and they highly value meat, although they don't have a lot of access to meat these days, so the beliefs about cannibal witches are tied up in this valuation of meat.

One man that this anthropologist Helen Regis interviewed talked about, "Oh, wouldn't it be great to be a cannibal witch? You could eat a plateful of intestines every day," and then he quickly corrected himself and said, "But I would never do that; I would never go that route," but it shows that there's this fear of cannibal witches because of this fear of their own passion, of wanting to eat meat, and of the ultimate rejection in some ways of the norms of pulaaku. If you gave in to eating human flesh, which the Fulbe say is the tastiest flesh of all, if you gave in to this base desire, you would really be rejecting all of the code of pulaaku. We have desire, we have envy, we have witchcraft, all wrapped up into one, and to be treated from an attack by a cannibal witch one has to go to the Mallum, the spiritual leader, the Koranic spiritual leader, who's going to protect you from this cannibal witch attack.

Less debilitating but more common than cannibal witch attacks are attacks by river spirits, and women are especially susceptible to this because Domaayo is located on the side of a river, and they will go down every day and collect water and bring it back up, and these river spirits can steal part of their soul. It's interesting that the Fulbe have a lot of lore about river spirits, and some of it ties in with tales about white engineers, French and English engineers who've come to Cameroon and started building roads as part of the development program in these remote regions of Cameroon. Regis quotes a story that was told to her by a man that she heard from several other people as well, about the relationship of these river spirits to the engineers who were building bridges over the rivers. Let me quote this; this is a Fulbe man:

"I hear it said that there are some whites who build bridges; then the spirits destroy them during the night. They bring out the engineers, the whites who know how to catch spirits. They say they capture the spirit—they say they catch it—and the spirit says, 'I leave you be.' They then release him, and they can go on with their construction. I learn that the spirits had captured a white man in Chad, not in Cameroon, strategically a distance away in Chad. Until now, the man is there. If they come with their binoculars, they see him captured. He's alive; he's in the water. Africans can see him too, but the whites have gadgets. They have binoculars they can look with, and they see him. The Africans don't have these tools. It's far, a thousand meters or so, a lot of water."

This is a wonderful story; it's a commentary on neo-colonial relations between whites and the Fulbes, and it also recognizes the power of the outside world, the power of these engineers, with their binoculars, with their technology, and also the power of the native spiritual world as well. It seems to be a morality tale, but paradoxically the morality is somewhat ambiguous here, and I think this reflects a fundamental ambiguity of many native peoples around the world, trying to work out their place in an increasingly globalized world.

Lecture Ten
Rites of Passage

Scope:

Most cultures around the world mark significant stages in the life cycle with rituals and celebrations. The most important of these rites of passage is when girls and boys become women and men. Such coming-of-age ceremonies are marked by a separation from the group, a transitional period in which normal social strictures are suspended, and a reintegration into the community as adults.

For Fulbe boys, the initiation ceremony occurs when they are between 7 and 12 years old. During a several-week-long "circumcision camp," boys are taken from their mothers, made to eat food considered unclean by Muslim practice to the point of vomiting, and physically pushed to the point of exhaustion—all the while being socialized in the stoic Fulbe code of manly behavior. Once they are circumcised, they reenter their communities as adult men.

A similar ceremony is performed by the Sambia of New Guinea, a culture marked by strong divisions between men and women. Among the Sambia, initiated boys will go to live in a communal men's house until they get married and have their first child; women, during their menstrual period, must stay in a menstrual hut outside the village. The Sambia believe that boys are born without semen and, thus, without manhood. During their initiation, boys are required to engage in ritualized homosexual behaviors in order to build up their manhood. We will see how these rituals relate back to Sambian origin myths and Freudian theories of development.

Outline

I. Every culture around the world recognizes important stages in the life cycle.

   A. Arnold van Genep in his pioneering *Rites of Passage* (1909) proposed a sequence for rite-of-passage ceremonies that holds well for many cultures.

   B. First, there is a separation of initiates from their families and the group.

1. During the ceremonial transition period, normal rules are often turned upside down. Victor Turner calls this a period of *liminality.* and notes that it produces a sense of bonding (or *communitas*) between the initiates.
2. Finally, the initiates are reintegrated into the society.

II. Male rites of passage among the Fulbe illustrate van Genep's model.

   A. Fulbe boys must be made into men through an initiation ceremony that culminates in their circumcision.
      1. During this ritual, they are instilled with the stoic principles of *pulaaku.*
      2. Before their initiation, boys have not had much contact with their fathers.

   B. The circumcision camp takes place when there is an adequate number of boys from about 7 to about 12 years old.
      1. The boys are separated from the village and taken to a makeshift camp on the far side of the river.
      2. The camp lasts only a few weeks but produces lifetime bonding among the boys and serves as an important symbolic break with the world of women.

   C. During the circumcision camp, the boys enter a stage of liminality where the normal rules that govern everyday life do not apply.
      1. They are made to eat road kill and other unclean foods. They are also made to eat excessively, to the point that they vomit.
      2. The boys endure physical hardships and punishments and are, finally, circumcised.

   D. The coming-in ceremony for the boys' return is an unusually festive time for the normally reserved Fulbe.
      1. A huge feast is thrown.
      2. The boys are paraded around as if they were sex objects, and the girls eye them with lust—behaviors that would ordinarily be severely punished.

III. The Fulbe mark four important phases in a woman's life.

   A. First is the status of "virgin," which lasts from birth until marriage. A virgin is not yet fully a woman.

B. After marriage, sometime between the ages of 12 and 14, a girl takes on the status of a married woman and is then considered to be a real woman.

C. After a divorce, a woman enters a liminal period and is known as a "free woman" until she marries again. Free women are seen as potentially dangerous because they have no man to control their sexuality.

D. After menopause, "old women" become more assertive and enjoy many more freedoms. They are no longer feared by men for their sexuality.

IV. The Sambia of Papua, New Guinea, also practice a dramatic coming-of-age ceremony for males.

   A. The Sambia, like the Fulbe, are a patrilineal society with a clear segregation between the sexes.

      1. Sambian communities have men's houses on the edge of the village. Women are not allowed to enter these houses.

      2. There are also menstrual huts located outside the village, where women must go during their periods.

      3. Houses are clearly divided between the men's side and the women's side, and there are even separate male and female paths through the villages.

   B. Boys are raised by their mothers until about age 7. They are seen as being potentially polluted and debilitated by such close contact with women and, thus, must be made into men through a series of rituals that will last until their first child is born, usually in their early 20s.

      1. Boys are not believed to be born with a supply of semen, which is closely linked to male virility. They are, thus, initiated by ingesting semen from older boys.

      2. This initiation reenacts the Sambian myth of Numboolyu and Chemchi, the two original beings, and provides an unusual resolution to the Oedipus complex.

      3. After the ritualized homosexual phase of initiation, adolescents are expected to marry women.

   C. The prolonged Sambian initiation process makes men suspicious and fearful of women. They often have difficulty moving from the men's hut and adjusting to living with their wives.

Readings:

Gilbert Herdt, *The Sambia*.

Victor Turner, *The Ritual Process*.

Thomas Gregor, *Anxious Pleasures*.

Questions to Consider:

1. What rights of passage are important in our own culture? What functions do these serve?

2. How do the conditions of Fulbe initiation forge bonds between the boys?

3. Why are severe male initiation rites associated with antagonistic relations between the sexes?

Lecture Ten—Transcript
Rites of Passage

Rites of passage are found in cultures around the world. They mark significant events in the life stage of an individual. In our own culture, we have birthdays, anniversaries, bar mitzvahs, bat mitzvahs, in some parts of the country debutante balls, various sorts of ceremonies that mark different life stages. But, in other cultures, these rites of passage often play a much more central role than they do in our own society. In this lecture, we're going to review theories of rites of passage and look to two case studies. First, returning to the Fulbe, we're going to look at male circumcision camps that change boys into men, and then we're going to turn to the Sambia of Highland Papua New Guinea and their most unusual rites of passage that mark the same transition.

The typology that we have for understanding rites of passage comes to us from the anthropologist Arnold van Genep, who published a book in 1909 titled *Rites of Passage*, and he noted that there are three main stages to rites of passage. The first is separation from a group. You take the individual who's going to go through this process out of the normal social group, take them away from the group; then you have a period of transition, and this period of transition might last a few minutes, a few days, a few weeks, even a number of years in extreme cases. You have a period of separation, a period of transition, and then reintegration back into the group, taking on this new stage of life, a boy becoming a man, a girl becoming a woman. The anthropologist Victor Turner published a landmark work in 1969 titled *The Ritual Process: Structure and Anti-structure*. In this book, basically what he did was theorize van Genep's middle stage, this stage of transition, and he gave it the term liminality.

In Turner's words, liminality is an ambiguous state of being; it's betwixt and between normal states or normal conditions. It mediates between inner desires and social controls. Turner, when he was writing about liminality, saw it present in all sorts of rituals, and he stressed that it's an inverse state, a situation of anti-structure, where normal social norms are reversed. The normal rules of social life don't apply during a liminal period; the world is literally turned upside down. What's normally forbidden is allowed; what you would normally do is forbidden during a period of liminality. For Turner, liminality symbolically represents a period of regression, away from culture and this ordered aspect of life and toward nature and the untamed chaos of nature. He said that it's a very important ritual for people to undergo because it allows them to get in touch with their natural sides and then reemerge and reaffirm the social order of things.

We can apply the concept of liminality not only to rites of passage but all sorts of other things. University students, for example, in the States are in this period of liminality. They're no longer children, they're not living at home with their parents, and yet they're not fully adults either. They're probably still relying on their parents for financial support. So we have these certain periods of liminality. Some scholars have argued that a problem in contemporary U.S. society is we don't have clearly marked rites of passage. It's not clear when a boy becomes a man or when a girl becomes a woman. We have all of these little steps along the way. At 16, an adolescent can get a driver's license; at 18, they can vote; at 21, they can buy alcohol, but there's never this one defining moment that says, "Yesterday you were a boy and today you're a man," or "Yesterday you were a girl and today you're a woman."

Turner and others have applied his concept of liminality to carnival celebrations, for example, carnival celebrations around the world, these moments when the normal social structure is turned upside down. It's a period of liminality. Where public drunkenness would normally be looked down upon, it's OK; where public nudity would be prohibited, it's allowed, the normal social order of things being turned upside down. Turner said that during carnival celebrations, for example, it serves this powerful collective psychological safety valve; it allows people to shed the shackles of the social order and to get back in touch with the untamed chaos of nature, and then on Ash Wednesday, after Mardi Gras, after carnival is over, then they can reintegrate and reaffirm the social order of things.

Turner also argued in talking about liminality that periods of liminality can induce what he termed *communitas*. Communitas is this feeling of tight solidarity, of group unity that's facilitated by collective liminality, so he said that when a group, especially when a group goes through a rite of passage and they have this period of liminality, it bonds the group together. Here we can think of hazing rituals in fraternities and sororities at universities, in the military. Various sorts of hazing rituals serve to bond groups together because the group undergoes a common hardship, this period where the normal order of things is turned upside down, and it creates solid bonds that can very often last a lifetime.

Getting back to the Fulbe initiation ceremonies and rites of passage, boys are the focus of the Fulbe initiation ceremony. When boys are growing up in Fulbe society, their fathers are very distant. They're taken care of by their mothers, they spend most of their time at home with their mothers, and their fathers are off with their male friends. A strong bond thus naturally emerges between boys and their mothers. But, keep in mind, this is a patriarchal society; this is a society where men are suspicious of women, where men see women as being potentially polluting, debilitating to the male, and so boys have to be taken away from women and this world of women and made into men somehow. It's a little bit dangerous for them to spend all of their time with their mothers and in the company of women.

The Fulbe men, they see women as potentially polluting; they're especially scared of menstrual blood. Menstruating women are not allowed to enter a mosque, for example, and so all of this pollution can rub off on the boys and this has to be cleansed away during the ritual process, the rite of passage. In Fulbe ideology, women and young children are also seen as being a bit pagan. Recall in the last lecture we talked about Levi-Strauss's dichotomy of nature and culture, and nature is to culture as chaos is to order, as naked is to clothed, as women are to men, and so forth; so women and children are seen to embody this unrestrained chaos of nature in some ways that men, who are seen as being more cultured, more civilized, are not, so they have to take the boys out of this women's world, cleanse them of any pollution they might have undergone, and make them into men.

What they do is they have a circumcision camp, as Regis calls it. It's an odd verbal image for me, a circumcision camp; when I think of camp, I think of Boy Scout camp or something, and this is very different, letters being written home, I would imagine, from the circumcision camp. Anyway, when there are enough boys in a village between the ages of seven and 12 years old, when there's a critical mass to form a cohort, these boys will be gathered up and taken out of the village to a camp set up on the far side of the river. The boys are separated from their families, literally taken out of their mother's arms sometimes, and housed in this camp across the river. The camp will last for several weeks, and in the camp the boys are forced to do all sorts of things that they would never do in everyday life. They enter this period of liminality; they've been separated from society and their mothers, and they enter this period of liminality.

During the camp, the boys will eat unclean animals, and they'll even eat roadkill, and as you're all aware, the Muslim tradition has very clear guidelines about what sorts of meats can be eaten. The boys are fed polluted meats, the meats that they're taught not to eat in Koranic school, and not just fed a little bit but they're fed so much that they get sick, and they throw up, and they vomit, and they're fed too much millet and they get sick. And so during this camp the normal rules are turned upside down. What they normally couldn't eat, they would eat. Where they would normally show restraint in pulaaku in not eating too much, they're forced to consume more than they normally would. So you have this situation where boys are separated from their mothers, they're breaking with the world of women, and put together in the circumcision camp, which creates a real sense of communitas between these boys, a sense of togetherness. They go through all the same hardships; they form a bond, and a bond that will last through the rest of their lives

The Fulbe circumcision camp basically follows the scheme put forth by van Genep: separation from the village, followed by a period of transition, what Turner would have called liminality; and then reintegration. The circumcision itself, in one way the focal point of the camp, the boys are being taken there to be circumcised, but in another sense it's an anti-climactic part of this process. The boys are taken apart one by one, and the foreskin of their penis is cut off, using sometimes a razor blade, sometimes a knife, sometimes a pair of scissors. It will be wrapped up with an herbal package and allowed to heal. It's not unlike in some ways female genital mutilation in other parts of Africa. Some symbolic anthropologists argue that cutting off the foreskin removes the female-looking part of the male genitalia, just as female circumcision removes the erectile tissue from the female anatomy, and so it's not only symbolically making them into men and women, it's physically making them into men and women, taking those parts of the anatomy that look like the other gender and permanently inscribing the symbolic statement on their body.

After they've undergone circumcision, they have a number of days to heal, and then there's reintegration back into Fulbe society. In this reintegration, after they've undergone the ceremony, there's a huge feast in the village that's thrown to welcome these boys, now men, back into society, and the boys are paraded around, almost as if they were brides or some sort of West African Chippendales, and the women are allowed to ogle and look at them with lust in their eyes. This is a carryover of this period of liminality. Normally women aren't supposed to show any sort of overt sexuality; it's dangerous. But in this coming-in ceremony, they're allowed to go around and ogle the boys who are being paraded around as new young men. And so there's an overt sexuality in this reintegration ceremony that would normally be opposed to everything in Fulbe society. But once they're reintegrated into society, their interaction with women ends. They will still though get married—marriage is very important for the Fulbe—but they won't spend a lot of time with their wives. They don't spend a lot of time with their mothers or sisters either.

Women in Fulbe society go to Koranic school, as do the men. The boys generally attend Koranic school until their late teens or early 20s, so they've gone through the circumcision camp between the time they're seven and 12 years old. They attend a Koranic school with their Mallum, learning to memorize the Koran and repeating the Koran verbatim, and boys will do this until their late teens or early 20s, and then they're allowed this period of license, where they can go out, and sometimes they leave their community, go to a big city, maybe drink alcohol, maybe experiment sexually. They're allowed this period of freedom, and then they are expected to come back to Islam, to come back to being devout Muslims in their late 30s and 40s and go on studying the Koran. That's basically the life cycle of a boy changing into a man in Fulbe society.

Here I'd like to mention the stages that women go through, that girls becoming women go through as well. In Fulbe life, the women have four distinct stages of life, four distinct life phases that they will hold. The first is that of a virgin, a young girl up until the age that she gets married, and girls get married between 12 and 14 years old. They often marry a much older man, and these virgins are seen as being pure, as being unformed, still a girl, not a woman yet, not as dangerous as a woman would be. Then after marriage, after she's been deflowered by her husband, she's no longer a girl, she's a woman, and she's betrothed. She might have a bit of say in who she marries, but not a whole lot; her family's really going to decide this for her. A 12-, 13-, 14-year-old girl really doesn't know who to marry anyway, one could argue. The marriage is presumptively, at the beginning anyway, for a lifetime; yet most women in Fulbe society get divorced. The average woman has 2.6 husbands in Fulbe society, and women can initiate these divorces. If the husband doesn't give enough cloth at the annual exchanges, doesn't give enough good cloth, only gives print cloth and not wax cloth, these are perfectly acceptable grounds for a woman to divorce her husband.

When a woman gets divorced, she enters into the third stage of her life, and that is the status of a free woman. Free women, they're women who have been divorced and in between marriages; they're probably going to get married again, and they're considered to be very dangerous beings by the Fulbe men. They're more subject to their passions than men are. Men are considered to be more disciplined in regards to sexuality, and this really turns upside down our own Western cultural model of men and women. We would assume that men have this unrestrained sexuality and that women are more reserved. Among the Fulbe, it's women who would be nymphomaniacs if they didn't have a man, if they didn't have a husband to keep them in their place, so men are scared of these free women, these divorced women. They have no husband to control them, and sometimes they have affairs. They will have affairs with younger men or with married men sometimes.

Eventually they'll get married again. As I've said, they get married two to three times generally during their lifetime. So you have the stage of virginity, and then a girl-woman is married, and then after she gets divorced she can be a free woman; and then finally after menopause, when they can no longer have children, they become asexual in a way. They're seen as not being as tied to the passions of nature as they once were, not as potentially dangerous as they once were, but seen as being wise, as someone who's lived through all of the travails that a woman, a mother, a wife has to live through. Very often they return to studying the Koran at this stage. They stopped, you'll remember, when they got married at 12 or 13 or 14 years old, they stopped going to Koranic school, but after they become these old women, they can go back to the Koran, and often they're seen as elders. People will go to them for advice, and people sometimes feel able to talk to them in a way that they couldn't talk to elder men.

Continuing this discussion of rites of passage, I'd like to turn to a group known as the Sambia, who live in Papua New Guinea, the Highlands of New Guinea. New Guinea, you'll remember, is off the coast of Australia. The Highlands are a very ragged territory, high elevations, seven or eight or nine thousand feet high, dramatic peaks and valleys, so you have lots of little groups that are geographically separated and don't have a lot of contact with one another, and, as a result, there are literally hundreds of languages, not just dialects, but hundreds of languages spoken in New Guinea, and the Sambia speak an Anga language. The Sambia are made famous by a number of studies conducted by the anthropologist Gilbert Herdt. He started going there in the late 1960s and early 1970s, and he's kept going back year after year, even to this day.

The Sambia is a pseudonymous name; the name of the group is well known among people who live in the area, but Herdt wanted to protect their privacy and to protect them from the curious tourists because of their unusual rituals, which we will talk about in just a moment. The Sambian, they live in Highland New Guinea. It's a tropical climate; they get about 150 inches of rainfall every year. The seasons, they have two seasons, rainy and dry. It's a region where there are these hundreds of groups divided by rough geography, divided by language, and you get lots of warfare and conflict between the different groups. In Sambian society, you also find a strong division between the spheres of men and women. They're not Muslim, so this isn't an Islamic division—it's not based on Islamic scripture—but men and women are even more segregated in Sambian society than they are in Fulbe society.

In a Sambian village, you have the village proper, and then on the outside of the village, there'll be a men's house—a clubhouse, we could call it—and this is where the men go and live when they start their initiation ceremony, and they'll actually live there from the time they're seven years old until their early 20s, sometimes their mid-20s. They'll live in this men's hut, live communally only with other men, until their first child is born. You have a village—on the outside is a men's hut. Inside the village, there's a central plaza area and circular houses around it, and inside these houses, these huts, will live a nuclear family, a man, his wife, and their children, but even inside the hut there's literally lines very often in the middle of the hut, and women cannot enter the man's side of the hut, so the women's side in the hut is when you first go in the door. A man would walk in, step over the woman's side of the hut, and enter his own side of the area.

So you have the men's clubhouses, the village proper, and then outside the village as well you'll have a menstrual hut and this is where women who are menstruating have to go during their periods. They leave the village, they leave their family, and they go out and they stay in this menstrual hut during their period. There's a strict segregation of men and women in the Sambian villages, and concerning these menstrual huts, there's been conflicting reports about whether they're—at first they were seen as a very bad thing for women. What an awful way of subjugating women; these men are forcing women to leave their homes when they're having their period and go out and live in these menstrual huts. Some recent revisionist research has suggested, however, that the women don't mind this at all. A woman's daily life in Sambian society is not easy: waking up at four in the morning; starting a fire; cooking food for the family; when breakfast is over starting to cook lunch. It's a very grueling lifestyle, and this is a chance for women to get together outside of the watchful eye of men and spend some leisurely time. And so is the segregation of women into a menstrual hut, is this an ugly side of patriarchy or is it a way in which women can live their lives a little better? The evidence is conflicting on this.

But getting back to the segregation of the sexes in Sambian villages, there are even separate paths through the village for men and women. Men walk on one path and women walk on another. I bring this up just to reinforce how divided men and women are in Sambian society. Men in Sambian society are expected to embody a quality that they call *jerungdu*, and this means fierceness. Historically, there have been a lot of battles between these groups in Highland New Guinea, and they value warriors. The men need to become warriors, and so they want to instill them with this sense of jerundu or fiercety, fierceness. And they do this through the initiation process.

Initiation for Sambian boys starts around the age of seven years old, about the same time that it starts for Fulbe boys, but for the Sambian boys initiation is not completed until their mid-20s, until the birth of their first child, and so it's this really long period of initiation, and throughout this whole period they will live in the men's house, live away from the women. During initiation, the boys are taken out of the village in a ceremony, again not unlike the Fulbe ceremony, where they're ripped out of their mother's arms. The mothers very often are screaming, "Don't take my child away. Don't take my son away," and the older men and the older boys come and they take these boys away. The boys don't know what's going to happen, so they're incredibly scared, and you take them out to a temporary camp set up outside of the village.

When the boys are in this camp, they're put through incredible hardships. They're made to dance for hours and hours on end. They're made to take long hikes. They're not given enough to eat. They're really pushed to the edge of consciousness, not unlike the way in which certain religious sects brainwash their converts, really pushing them to the edge of consciousness so that the mind opens up and is willing to accept all of these new things and internalize these new ways of looking at the world. Among the Sambia, unlike in Fulbe initiation, the initiation process is supposed to be very secret. The women in society aren't supposed to know what goes on; there are these huge secrets. Gilbert Herdt, the anthropologist who has worked there, calls them screaming secrets because the women actually know what goes on, but they can't talk about it. They have to act like they don't know what's going on, so the boys are taken out of their homes, away from their mothers, and they're put in these camps where they learn the secrets of manhood.

In these initiation camps, they learn how to play flutes, and with these flutes, and these are secret flutes—the women aren't supposed to see these flutes—with these flutes, the boys, they're made to play the flutes, they're hit on the head with the flutes, and then the flutes are used as a prelude for teaching them the basis of Sambian initiation, and this really has to be one of the most unusual rituals ever observed by anthropologists in the world, and it is ritualized homosexuality between the older boys and men and these younger boys. To understand a Sambian initiation here, we have to go over a bit of Sambian ethnobiology. The Sambian believes that men are not born with a supply of semen and that they don't produce it themselves. Instead, the men are born with an empty organ called a *tingu*, and the semen has to somehow get built up in the body, and the semen is the source of *jerungdu*, of fierceness.

It's crucially important for boys to develop, healthy physically and psychologically and socially, that they undergo this process, that they undergo this insemination, and so the young boys are forced— they're taught—to perform fellatio, oral sex, on the older boys, and they do this because they really believe that the young boys don't have any semen, and so they have to ingest this from the older boys so that they can grow up and become a strong man. The Sambia will tell you, "Of course it works. Look, we take these prepubescent boys, and they undergo this process, and in a couple of years their genitals start growing, they start getting pubic hair, so it obviously works."

The justification for this ritual goes back to the origin myth in Sambian society, which boys don't learn until the very last stage of initiation, when they're in their mid-20s, after their first child has been born. The Sambian initiation myth says that in the beginning, there were two individuals, Numboolyu and Chemchi, and these were basically asexual beings. They both had incipient genitalia of both sexes, but it wasn't very highly developed. Over time, what happened was Chemchi began performing fellatio on Numboolyu, and Numboolyu became a man and Chemchi grew larger breasts and became a woman. Over time, and the Sambia believe that a woman can become impregnated either through intercourse or through oral sex as well by ingesting semen, they believe that Chemchi got pregnant, and then Numboolyu, when she came to term, cut an opening in her which became the vagina, and she gave birth to a child, so we have this first couple, Numboolyu and Chemchi, the Sambian Adam and Eve, although they're definitely eating from a different apple tree than our Adam and Eve ate from.

They have a son, and they have another son a few years later, and when the older son starts going through puberty he comes to his father and he says, "I have these feelings. I have an erection. I don't know what to do with it. Why can't I have sex with Chemchi, my mother, your wife?" Numboolyu, the father, says "No way, that's totally out of the question," so we have this classic Oedipal conflict reflected in the Sambian mythology, a boy wanting to have sex with the mother, the father not allowing that to happen, the father prohibiting that. But the Sambia have come up with this unique solution to the Oedipal conflict, and that is, the father Numboolyu told the older boy to have his younger brother perform oral sex on him so that it would both serve as a sexual outlet for the older boy and build up the seminal fluids in this organ, the *tingu* of the younger boy.

Throughout their lifetime, males have to be very careful about not wasting their semen. They have to be very possessive toward their semen, and women are seen as being semen-hungry, so men have to be careful around women, about having sex with women. They don't want to have sex too often because the women are going to soak up all of your semen, and if this life source is depleted, a man can die; so after the Sambia have sex, they will actually go out and lick the sap of this particular tree to help them rebuild their semen supply.

When they're away during this camp, at the beginning of initiation, they learn to perform these homosexual activities. Gilbert Herdt, who's worked with them, calls it ritualized homosexuality, and it's important to point out that most of the boys don't want to do this; they're forced to do this. It's something that they are embarrassed about, they don't want to talk with the women about, and very often they don't even want to talk to anthropologists about this process at all. The elders are forcing them to do it, and through the initiation process they haven't been fed much, they've been dancing all night, they've been taken on these long hikes, they're really pushed to the edge of consciousness, and they're very susceptible to internalizing these new ideas. This goes on for a period of time.

Once boys enter into puberty, they become the active partner in this relationship of oral sex with younger boys. They will eventually get married in their late teens or early 20s, and they go through a period of bisexuality, where they're still living in the men's house where these ritualized homosexual acts are performed, and they start having sex with their wives as well. We have this transition, this fairly unique transition of homosexuality, bisexuality, and then men are expected to become fully heterosexual after the birth of their first child.

This is an unusual ritual, but it's not out of the question. There are other groups in Papua New Guinea who practice similar sexual practices. There are groups in Amazonia, although they don't have this ritualized homosexual aspect, they do have menstrual huts; they have secret men's cults and so forth. While this is an extreme example, the same general sort of pattern of antagonism between the sexes holds in a number of different cultures. These rites of passage, marking a transition from childhood to adulthood—and in most cultures this is a defining feature of becoming an adult, is getting married and having a family, and this is going to be the topic of our next lecture.

Lecture Eleven
Family, Marriage, and Incest

Scope:

All cultures practice some form of marriage, if we define marriage rather broadly. Arrangement marriages are the norm around the world, with romantic love seen as a weak basis for a lifetime partnership. The most casual form of marriage comes from the Nayar of India, where women have a number of "visiting" husbands," yet even here males are required to publicly recognize their relationships and claim paternity for their children. Many cultures favor cousin marriages—making children marry outside of the immediate family, but not too far outside that family relations get diluted. Nonetheless, even among cultures with such marriage rules, in practice we find a degree of flexibility in choosing a spouse.

In a majority of cultures, men may have more than one wife, although usually it is a small percentage of males who can afford to support multiple wives. About 15% of cultures practice monogamy, or serial monogamy, as is the case in the West. The rarest form of marriage (found in only six cultures) is polyandry, where a woman has more than one husband. Polyandrous marriages are generally found in extreme environments (for example, on the Himalayan highlands of Nepal), where it is advantageous to limit population growth.

While romantic love is often not seen as a valid basis for marriage, it is found in virtually all cultures. All cultures also enforce a prohibition on incest—the fundamental restrictions on whom one may marry. We find that the range of what are considered incestuous relations varies significantly.

Outline

I. In less complex societies, kinship serves as the basis for economic, political, and other social roles.

    A. There are two primary types of kinship relations, *consanguines* (blood relatives) and *affines* (in-laws). These are biological and legal relations, but their significance is culturally constructed.

B. Descent is the intergenerational relationship between consanguines. Descent groups serve important social functions but vary in size and composition.

    1. *Lineages* are groups of consanguines who can trace their relationships back to a known common ancestor.

    2. *Clans* are groups of lineages that claim common descent from a mythical ancestor.

II. There are three main forms of descent groups: patrilineal, matrilineal, and cognatic. These determine paths of inheritance, as well as social roles in society.

    A. About 40 percent of all societies practice patrilineal descent, in which relations are traced through male lines.

        1. Patrilineal descent is associated with patriarchal societies. Even where the ideology of male dominance is muted, however, women in patrilineal systems often live their lives as outsiders.

        2. In a patrilineal system, one simply does not feel related to one's mother and her family as one does with the father's side of the family. Sisters are members of their father's patrilineage, but their children belong to their husband's patrilineage.

    B. Matrilineal systems are much rarer, found in only about 15 percent of all societies.

    C. The most common form of descent is cognatic descent, in which relationships are traced through both male and female lines. About 45 percent of all societies practice cognatic descent.

        1. Cognatic descent is associated with mobility and is, generally, a much more flexible system. It is practiced in most modern Western cultures, as well as in smaller-scale societies around the world.

        2. The Dobe Ju/'hoansi, a nomadic band–level society in the Kalahari region of southern Africa, practice cognatic descent, which helps them maintain large networks of kin to call on in times of need.

III. Monogamy is relatively rare cross-culturally. Most cultures allow men to have multiple wives, and a very few permit multiple husbands.

A. About 82 percent of societies allow polygyny, the marriage of one man to multiple women.

  1. Having multiple wives is a sign of wealth and prestige.

  2. There are also clear political and economic benefits to having more than one wife.

  3. Trobriand chiefs strategically marry a number of wives from different lineages in order to increase their political networks.

B. There have only been about five reported cases of societies that are polyandrous, with women having more than one husband.

  1. Polyandry appears to emerge in harsh physical circumstances with extremely limited resources and a need for low population growth.

  2. Tibetans in Nepal practice fraternal polyandry, in which brothers will marry a single wife. This prevents family lands from being broken up.

IV. Marriage, in some form or another, is found in all cultures.

A. Evolutionarily, human beings are predisposed to pair-bonding. Given the incredible helplessness of human infants, it has, until recently, been a biological imperative to have two caregivers.

B. Most Americans marry for love, although this is the exception rather than the rule around the world.

  1. Some historians and social scientists believe that the notion of romantic love is a Western ideology first developed by 12th-century French troubadours.

  2. A survey I conducted of 166 cultures found some form of romantic love in all of them. Perhaps, then, some have speculated, there may be a biological predisposition to falling in love.

C. Although pair-bonding may be universal, the precise form of marriage varies greatly. The most extreme example comes from the Nayar of southern India, who practice two types of marriage.

1. When girls reach their early teenage years there, they participate in *tali-rite marriages*. The couple will cohabitate for only a few days or weeks, and the marriage may or may not be consummated. Few obligations follow this initial ceremonial period.
2. Women then enter into multiple *sandbadham marriages*. These are fairly casual unions; the couples do not live together, and a woman may maintain any number of these relationships at one time. Despite this openness, when a child is born, it is crucial that a man claim paternity.

V. Even though romantic love appears to be a cultural universal, arranged marriages are by far the norm in societies around the world.

VI. Just as marriage is found in all cultures, so too are restrictions on whom one can marry. Incest taboos may appear as a sort of natural law, but their precise formulation varies from culture to culture.

A. In the Judeo-Christian tradition, incest rules go back to prohibitions spelled out in Leviticus. These were greatly expanded by the Catholic Church in the 12th century.

B. Incest taboos may have a biological basis in that they avoid the ill effects of recessive genetic traits, although inbreeding would also have weeded out such traits over the long term.

C. Edward Westermark argued that familiarity breeds contempt and, thus, that children raised together would lose sexual passion for one another. Several studies seem to bear out his hypothesis.
1. On *kibutzim* in Israel where children were raised together, virtually no members of the same cohort married one another.
2. Very poor Chinese families sometimes practice infant betrothal with their daughters in what are called *sim-pua marriages*; the future husband and wife grow up together in the same manner as siblings. These marriages have low fertility rates and high divorce rates.

Readings:

Jack Goody, *The Development of the Family and Marriage in Europe*.

Arthur Wolf, *Sexual Attraction and Childhood Association*.

Yolanda Murphy and Robert Murphy, *Women of the Forest*.

Helen Fisher, *Anatomy of Love: A Natural History of Mating*.

Melvyn C. Goldstein, "When Brothers Share a Wife," *Natural History*, March 1987, pp. 39–48.

Questions to Consider:

1. What evolutionary pressure would promote pair-bonding?
2. Is incest a natural aversion or is it learned?
3. Why is polygyny so common and polyandry so rare around the world?

Lecture Eleven—Transcript
Family, Marriage, and Incest

Today I'd like to talk about marriage and the family, both of these as the nucleus of social relationships. Kinship, which is the culturally recognized relationships based on blood and on marriage, has long been a staple of anthropology, something we've been concerned with. Your own kinship system probably seems natural to you. We were raised from earliest age to learn our kinship terms. Your father's brother is of course your uncle; your mother's sister is of course your aunt. But in many societies around the world, your father's brother would be called father; your mother's sister might be called mother; you might have a number of relatives that you would call brother and sister that aren't what we would consider to be your biological brothers and sisters.

We generally take kinship terms to be the equivalent of biological relationships, and kinship terms do try and represent biological relationships, but it's important to keep in mind that the anthropological concept of kinship is concerned with these cultural models of relatedness, and they overlap with biological relationships, but they're distinct in certain ways. It's a model, it's a scheme, it's a cultural model, as we've talked about in previous lectures. In this lecture, we're going to review different sorts of kinship structures, lineages and clans; matrilineal, patrilineal, and cognatic societies; and then we're going to turn to marriage, romantic love, and the universal prohibition against incest.

I would like for you to keep in mind during this lecture that the rules of kinship, like any role of culture, like any rule of language in fact, they're always flexible, they're always changing. We're improvising, based on these rules, and changing them, based on the situations in which we find ourselves, so as we talk about them, these rules may seem hard and fast. In practice, they're very often much more flexible. We have two main types of kinship that we distinguish in anthropology, consanguineal kin and affinal kin. Consanguineal comes from consanguines, and the Latin root for blood, sanguine, and it refers to blood relatives. Affinal kin, what we would call our in-laws, refers to relatives by marriage rather than by blood. We also have fictive kin, godparents, for example, or family friends who we might call aunt or uncle or even brother or sister that don't have any sort of biological relationship.

Consanguines are called descent groups, and descent groups have lots of important functions in societies that don't have formal legal structures, formal economic systems. Descent groups can regulate marriage; they often serve as economic units holding land in common, for example. They even serve religious functions, as certain rituals will be passed down from generation to generation in a descent group. There are two main types of descent groups. The first is clans, and the second is lineages, and the big difference between these is that clans trace their common origin back to a mythical ancestor and lineages trace their origin back to a known ancestor, so they both believe that they're descended from a common ancestor, but in lineages you know who that person is, and in a clan it's very often a mythical figure. Clans are very often made up of groups of lineages; they're larger than lineages.

There are several types of descent groups. The first we can talk about is patrilineal descent groups. In patrilineal societies, and they make up about 40 percent of societies around the world, everyone is related through the males. Descent is traced only through male lines; the chain of descent always stops with the female, so in a patrilineal society you're not really related to your mother and your mother's side of the family in the same way that you're related to your father and your father's side of the family. This seems odd to us because we see ourselves as being related equally to both sides of our family, but not in patrilineal societies, and relatives are conceived in different ways as well. Mother's brother, whom we would call an uncle, mother's brother, an uncle, is a very different sort of relative in a patrilineal society than your father's brother, also whom we would call uncle. So we have patrilineal descent groups.

We also have matrilineal descent groups, which, as the name implies, descent is traced through female lines. There's a much smaller percentage of societies in the world that are matrilineal, only about 15 percent, so it's fairly rare, and here descent always stops with the male. For example, a man's children are not members of his own matrilineage; they're not members of his family in this cultural model. They're members of their mother's family. In matrilineal societies, ironically, it's not women who really run things. If women ran a society, we would call that a matriarchy. Where descent is traced through female lines, we call this matrilineality, and we have 15 percent of those societies are matrilineal, but in none of these do women hold the formal positions of power, so they're not matriarchies. Men still are the chiefs; they hold the formal positions of authority and power in these societies. There's no recorded case of a matriarchy in the ethnographic record.

So I have patrilineal societies, matrilineal societies, and finally cognatic societies, and this is the system that our own culture uses. We're neither matrilineal nor patrilineal; we trace our relationships through both the mother's side of the family and the father's side of the family. Generally, you have the possibility in our own society, in a cognatic society, of feeling equally related to your mother's side and your father's side of the family. Cognatic descent is found in about 45 percent of the world's cultures, and it's the most flexible system. It's obviously a lot more flexible than matrilineality or patrilineality and it's often associated with mobility, and so, strangely enough, it unites gathering and hunting groups, nomadic groups who need a very flexible kinship system, and industrial and post-industrial societies like our own. We'll come back to these in this lecture and in later lectures, but right now I want to move on to marriage for a moment.

Why do people get married? It seems obvious to us. You get married because you fall in love; you find your one true-life partner, fall madly in love and get married, and hopefully live happily ever after. But for most of the people in the world, marrying for love, marrying for these romantic notions that we hold so dear as Westerners, is not seen as a valid reason. Love is seen as a youthful folly in many cultures, something fickle, whereas marriage is the ultimate contract, a lifetime bond between individuals, and not only between individuals but between families as well. In many cultures around the world, love is not seen as a good reason for getting married, and when marriage is occurring at such an early age—you'll remember that among the Fulbe, girls get married when they're 12, 13, or 14 years old—maybe they're not capable of choosing their best partner.

This seems odd to us. Who would know better than I who I should marry? But if you're 12, 13 or even 14, 15, 16, 17 years old, how do you know who your best spouse is going to be for the rest of your life? These kids have no idea. Their hormones are raging wildly, they have these crazy romantic notions in their head, so the parents think that they should choose who their children's spouses should be. It's not just a question of personal choice. The idea of monogamy is not the norm in marriage customs around the world.

A number of historians and anthropologists believe that romantic love is a Western invention. This is actually probably the standard view in history and in anthropology as well, that romantic love arose in the 11th and 12th century France, in the courtly culture where there were all of these troubadours and the immensely wealthy courts of the time, all these people just hanging around the court with all of this leisure time, and so the men and the women, to divert themselves, came up with this idea of romantic love, and men started falling in love with women and writing love poetry and so forth, and the women started falling in love with men. The vocabulary of romantic love really entered in the popular discourse at this time.

I did some research about 10 years ago with my co-author, Bill Jankowiak, looking for evidence of romantic love in cultures around the world, and we took a sample of 168 cultures and we read everything we could find about these cultures, looking for evidence of romantic love. It's hard to find, because in most cultures they practice arranged marriage, so people aren't marrying for romantic love, so we had to look for things like suicides of unrequited love and elopements or love poetry, and in the study we found evidence of romantic love in 90 percent of the societies that we looked at, 90 percent, and in the other 10 percent it was very often probably a case of ethnographers overlooking or not including the data that we needed to make a determination.

So a number of sociobiologists picked up on this finding to argue that perhaps romantic love evolved early on in hominid evolution to facilitate pair-bonding and perhaps there is some biological basis for feelings of romantic love, the function that would be to create a pair bond, to facilitate raising of children, and some studies have shown in recent years that when people are in love there are elevated levels of dopamine and other hormones, and so there are actually physical chemical changes that occur in the brain when one falls in love. An interesting thing is, researchers at first thought that they would find the brain waves of people in love would look like obsessive-compulsives, people suffering from obsessive-compulsive disorder, and what they actually found is, when they do these brain scans, PET scans and MRIs and so forth, that the brain patterns of people in love, deeply in love, look more like coke addicts than they do like obsessive-compulsives, and so perhaps there's this addictive quality to love as well that evolved to help us form pair-bonds.

Monogamy is the exception in cultures around the world rather than the rule. Most cultures allow some form of polygamy, of multiple spouses. Let me make a clarification here about the terminology that we're using. Polygamy is the overarching term, and it means having more than one spouse, a man having more than one wife or a woman having more than one husband. In anthropology, we use two more precise terms: polygyny, which refers to a man having more than one wife; and polyandry, which is when a woman has more than one husband. Both polygyny and polyandry are forms of polygamy. Polygyny is very common around the world; about 82 percent of the world's societies allow men to have more than one wife. But, on the other hand, polyandry is extremely rare. We only know six or seven cases, less than one percent of the cultures that have been sampled in the world practice polyandry. It's extremely rare, and it seems to be most closely associated with extreme environmental conditions.

The best known example is of the ethnic Tibetans living in Nepal, a very rough environment, 12,000 feet above sea level. Most of the families are poor and have very little cultivatable land, and they practice a very specific form of polyandry in which brothers share a single wife, and this is called fraternal polyandry, when brothers share a single wife. Why might this be? They live in this harsh environment, not a ton of land to go around, and fraternal polyandry keeps land together. These men are marrying the same woman, so they can all farm the same land. They compose a single household, and, too, it reduces the rate of reproduction. Women are limited in the number of children that they can have in their lifetime, and if one woman has several husbands, the absolute rate of reproduction will be very low.

Marriage is generally considered to be a human universal; people in all cultures bond with members of the opposite sex, but there are a few exceptions, and actually the exception that might prove the rule in this case is a group called the Nayar, and we find them in southwest India. They're the example that's often held up to show that marriage is not universal, but even among the Nayar we find bonding between men and women, something that looks a lot like marriage and is very important to their culture. The Nayar are matrilineal; they're a matrilineal society. The core of the household is a brother and sister, or brothers and sisters, and they will live together and have their lands and their houses in common. Traditionally, the Nayar have been a very warlike society. The men are warriors. They would go off for long periods of time and fight and then come back periodically to their own households.

Among the Nayar, we find two forms of what we can call marriage. The first is called a tali-rite, and this is basically a rite of passage, a puberty rite, a coming-of-age ceremony for girls, much more so for girls than boys. When a girl is somewhere between the ages of seven and 12, very often prepubescent, before she's begun her menstrual cycle, she will marry a man who lives in the same village and who's been selected by her parents, but this man should be from another matrilineage. They will cohabit for a few days. The man has the right to have sex with this wife, but they don't always do it. Especially if the girl is very young, the man will not have sex with his wife, but once the girl has gone through this cohabitation, whether she's had sex or not, before she goes through it she's a girl and when she comes out she's a full woman, she's a real woman in Nayar society, and in fact is called by the term that they use for women, the honorific term for women. This marriage, this tali-rite marriage, might only last for three, four, or five days, but it's an important part of making girls into women.

Afterwards, when a girl gets older, she's going to have very little to do with this first husband, this tali-rite husband. There are a few points in the life cycle where they have to get back together, and the husband will give certain ritual gifts to his wife, but for the most part this is a three- to five-day marriage, if you will, and then it ends there. But afterward, when the girl gets older, she can enter into another form of marriage, which we call sandbadham marriages, and these are marriage based on mutual consent. They're not arranged marriages, and they also have this serial quality. Sandbadham husbands are also called visiting husbands, and what they'll do is, after dinner—and you'll remember that men are living with their sisters in their family household—a man will leave his home after

©2004 The Teaching Company Limited Partnership

dinner, go to his sandbadham wife, put his spear in front of the doorway to let other people know that he's there. He'll spend the night with his wife and then leave the next morning and go back to his sister's house, where he'll eat and have breakfast.

A woman can have various sandbadham marriages at one time, up to 20, for example, and most women have two, three, four or five—up to 10, 20 is very unusual—but they can have multiple sandbadham marriages at the same time. In some ways, these are very casual relationships, and they can be terminated without any legal recourse, and people don't seem to really get upset. They can be ended by mutual consent in that way. The visiting husbands, sandbadham husbands, will give things to their wives, some cooking oil, maybe a little bit of money, not too much, but a little bit to help them get by in their everyday lives. The women don't depend on their husbands for their survival, but it's a nice little extra bit that he gives them.

The crucial thing occurs when a woman gets pregnant. Every child has to have a father in Nayar society. Paternity has to be acknowledged, but if a woman has eight sandbadham husbands, for example, how does she know who the father is? We can always be sure of maternity, but we can never (at least in the days before DNA testing), we could never be absolutely sure of paternity, and what happens is one of the husbands has to step up to the plate and claim to be the father of this child. Often a lot of negotiation goes on between the woman and her sandbadham husbands, getting them to claim paternity in this case. Marriage among the Nayar is not exclusive. The couples don't cohabitate; it's a very different form of marriage than our own form. However, it's very important. This form of marriage, both the tali-rite and the sandbadham, are very important in Nayar society, and it's important to validate paternity, to show who the father of a child is, and this is a common thread in marriage and cultures throughout the world, claiming paternity.

I'd like to move on at this point and talk just a bit about incest. Incest is based around rules of exogamy. Exogamy is marrying outside of a particular group, and endogamy, endogamy is marrying within a particular group. One of the universal taboos found in cultures around the world is a prohibition against incest, against having sexual relationships or marrying some category of kin. You have to marry outside of a given group; you have to marry exogamously. But the rub is, what that category of kin is changes and varies significantly from society to society. In our own culture, whom one can marry varies from state to state. First-cousin marriage is prohibited in most states, I believe all states, and in some states second-cousin marriage is prohibited as well, although not that long ago there were a lot of first- and second-cousin marriages, even in our own culture.

Interestingly, we generally take a revulsion about incest to be natural. It's disgusting; why would anybody want to do that? It's just one of those perversities of everyday life. But, as I said, the range of what we consider to be incestuous has changed over time. The universal prohibition against incest is just with one's siblings, one's parents and one's children, so just the basic nuclear family, what we would consider to be the nuclear family. This is the universal prohibition against incest; no culture in the world allows marriage or sexual relationships within this group. I have to admit, there are couple of very rare exceptions, Hawaiian nobility, Egyptian kings and queens, this idea that where royalty is descended from the gods and the bloodline has to be kept pure, they allow brother and sister to marry occasionally, but these are very rare cases, and for the most part every culture in the world prohibits sexual relations between brothers and sisters and parents and children.

But the range of incestuous relatives is culturally defined. Is first-cousin marriage incestuous? Most people would agree. What about second-cousin marriage? Most people would still agree, but where do we draw the line? At what point does incest start? In the Western tradition, our prohibitions against incest come from the Judeo-Christian tradition, come from the Bible, in particular Chapter 18 in Leviticus, verse 6, and in parts of Chapter 20 of Leviticus as well, where we find a number of prohibitions listed. For example, do not dishonor your father by having sexual relations with your mother. She is your mother; do not have relations with her. Do not have sexual relations with your sister and so forth, but this isn't a very wide range of relatives that are prohibited. One is not supposed to have sexual relations with parents, with aunts or uncles, with grandchildren and so forth, but it's a very narrow range of what is explicitly prohibited in Leviticus.

But beyond that, the Catholic Church started expanding out what was considered to be incestuous, and in A.D. 385, Pope Theodeus I prohibited first-cousin marriage. This wasn't prohibited in the Bible, it wasn't found in the scripture, but the Pope decided that that was a little bit too close and prohibited it, and then gradually the Catholic Church expanded out the range of what was considered to be incestuous so that by A.D. 1059, Pope Nicholas II prohibited marriage to the seventh degree. That means you couldn't marry— you would have your father, your grandfather, your great-grandfather, great-great-grandfather, great-great-great-grandfather, great-great-great-great-grandfather, great-great-great-great-great-grandfather, and any of their descendants would be prohibited from marriage. If you're living in rural France in the 11th century, you can't marry anybody; nobody in your village would be eligible to be married.

But of course there was an exception. You could buy a dispensation from the church; you could buy the right to marry your second cousin or your third cousin or even your first cousin, so one intent, whether it was intentional or not, of the Catholic Church's expansion of the incest prohibition was an increase in the sales of dispensations, of licenses to break canonical law. The range of what was considered to be incestuous was gradually shrunk back in the Catholic tradition. In 1215, it was reduced to four degrees. In 1537, it was reduced to two degrees. It was reduced for South American Indians first and then later for descendants of Africans. In 1917, it was reduced to two degrees, and finally it was reduced to two degrees for everyone in the world.

But some sort of prohibition against incest is found in all cultures, and why might this be? The obvious answer that comes to mind is inbreeding. We don't marry our relatives because of the dangers of having recessive genes come to the fore. There's one study that has found that the children of very close incestuous relationships are eight times more likely to be born with birth defects. This is true, but it doesn't help us understand why there are different cultural conceptions of what is incest, why the group that is considered incestuous varies from culture to culture. Is marrying your second cousin incest? What if your second cousin was adopted? Would that be incest? Most people would still consider it to be incest, but it's adopted, so there's not a biological relationship there, so incest is cultural; it's a social prohibition. Inbreeding is a partial answer, but it's an incomplete explanation for fully explaining incest taboos.

The scholar Edward Westermark offered another explanation, and he coined the phrase "familiarity breeds contempt," and this is from his 1891 work *The History of the Human Marriage*. What he means here is if you're raised with someone day in and day out, like a brother or sister, even if they're not your biological brother or sister, it's a turnoff. It's not romantic; sexual relationships won't flourish because growing up together mutes that kind of lust and sexuality. In the last decades, a few studies have been done that give support to the idea that familiarity breeds contempt, and the most famous were done in kibbutzim in Israel, kibbutzim, the communal communities in Israel that were started in the 1950s, and there were studies done in the 1960s and 1970s looking at marriage patterns and looking at sexual relationships between people who were raised on very traditional kibbutzim.

On these rigid kibbutzim, children would be raised in dormitories away from their parents. They would visit their parents every day, but they would be raised as a cohort away from their parents, so they were raised with this peer group, intimately seeing each other every day, boys and girls, men and women as they grow up. One study looked at 125 couples that had been raised since birth on the same kibbutz, and none of them got married to each other, none of them, and you'd say, "Who would you find for a potential mate?" The obvious example would be someone that you were living with day in and day out. This would be an obvious pool of potential marriage partners, but none of the people in the study married one another, and there have been other studies that show that there are very few sexual relations as well among youths on kibbutzim.

The other example I want to mention that moves toward proving this hypothesis that familiarity breeds contempt was done by the anthropologist Arthur Wolf. He worked with the Chinese exile community living in Taiwan, and he noticed that there was a prevalence of a certain type of marriage called the sim-pua marriage. The sim-pua marriage is infant betrothal. It's normally done by very poor families who can't afford to raise their child, especially a daughter, and so they betroth their daughter at a very early age, sometimes as early as six or seven months, sometimes as old as three or four years, but betrothing them to their future husband at a very early age. The girl then goes and lives with her future husband's family and is raised like a sister. They very often sleep in the same bed, they bathe together, they eat together; it's just like she becomes a daughter in this family, until she comes of age, and then she's expected to marry who she's been living with as a brother and live the rest of her life in marriage that way.

Arthur Wolf looked at these marriages to see how successful they were. He found that the fertility rate was 30 percent lower than other sorts of marriage, so something's going on here. The fertility rate was 30 percent lower. He started interviewing people who were in sim-pua marriages, and he found out that these marriages were incredibly tumultuous. The husbands were more likely to cheat on their wives; there were more avid consumers of prostitutes and pornography; there was lots of familial strife, domestic abuse, and a high rate of divorce. Wolf concludes that it's because familiarity breeds contempt; these children were raised with one another since infants, just as if they were brother and sister, and then when it came the moment to initiate the marriage, to have sexual relationships, both sides, the boys and the girls, very often refused. There are accounts of mothers having to use a broom and force the children into the bridal chamber to consummate this marriage.

Does incest have a biological basis? Probably, potentially. Are there also important cultural, psychological factors going on here as well? Most certainly. Does marriage have an evolutionary cause? Perhaps. To facilitate pair-bonding, it makes a lot of sense, but, as we've seen, marriage is conceived of very differently in cultures around the world. We have arranged marriages, we have these multiple spouses, we have these infant betrothals of the sim-pua marriage. Even our kinship terms, which seem so natural to us, are cultural constructions. Yes, they're based on biological relationships, but we extend that out to step siblings and adopted siblings and so forth, and so we see here the importance of culture. In the next lecture, we're going to apply these concepts of kinship and culture to the Trobriand Islanders.

Lecture Twelve
Multiple Spouses and Matrilineality

Scope:

Close to the agora of Athens lies the Ceramicus cemetery, where both private and public burials took place. In this lecture, we will examine not only attitudes toward death but also the practices associated with commemorating the dead. At the Ceramicus, more and more elaborate funerary sculptures were erected to memorialize the dead. Special attention was given to the young, in particular men who had died in battle on behalf of Athens. Eventually, the monuments grew so grand that the Athenians passed legislation limiting the amount of money that could be spent on funerary markers. Before the age of Pericles, burials had been marked by huge amphorae half buried in the ground. On them, we see scenes of the *prothesis*, or laying out of the body, and the *ekphora*, or funeral procession, in which the dead person was taken from the house to the burial ground. The expense of these ceremonies, as well as the graves themselves, testified to the status of the dead person's family. Death itself was regarded as a gloomy affair. Descriptions of the underworld make it sound dreary, and as in many cultures, the Athenians took pains to placate the spirits of the dead, afraid that otherwise, they might be haunted by them.

Outline

I. An encounter with the dead.

  A. In the *Odyssey*, Homer describes the visit of Odysseus to the underworld. In Hades, he meets some of the heroes he once knew in the Trojan War. When Achilles tells him that he would rather be the poorest day-laborer than king of all the dead, he expresses the Greek view of death.
    1. In general, the underworld was inhabited by souls who were described as uncaring or heedless.
    2. The only ghost to keep his wits was Teiresias the seer.
    3. Some evil-doers were actually punished, but dead spirits existed in a kind of limbo.

4. In Euripides's *Alcestis*, the heroine gives her life that her husband may live and was probably present on stage as an entirely mute ghost in the final act.

B. As in many cultures, the Greeks mingled respect and fear in their attitudes toward the dead. In fact, the dead received different treatment according to whether they were ordinary folk or heroes. In the case of ordinary folk, death and burial was generally simple. Funeral chambers and mounds were rarely used. Instead, simple inhumation or cremation was preferred. Both techniques existed in classical times.

    1. Before Pericles's time, Athens had already established an area largely given over to burial. This was the Ceramicus (Potters' Field), northwest of the agora.

    2. From 900 B.C. onward, the Athenians increasingly relied on simple pit inhumations.

    3. By 750 B.C., they were marking burials with large amphorae half buried at the head of the grave.

C. In the 5th century, burials in Athens were quite simple, with a few grave goods left in a small trench cut across the top of the grave. One distinctive form of pottery, the white-ground *lekythos*, is particularly associated with such burials. The markers naming the deceased were still also simple. Around 425, spending on burials and grave stelai increased dramatically. Most of the elaborate grave monuments to survive from Athens date from the late 5th century until legislation was introduced in 317 to curb spending; these monuments feature excellent sculpture in deep relief.

II. The change in commemoration practices is probably linked to the dramatic increase in casualties caused by the Peloponnesian War and the plague.

A. The most common motif on these monuments is the so-called *dexiosis*, or handshake. Some interpret this to be a reunion scene, looking forward to the time when the recently departed will be reunited with loved ones.

B. By the end of the 5th century, public and private commemoration took place side by side. Just beyond the Dipylon Gate, one entered the area called the most beautiful suburb of Athens. Here was located a *demosion sema*, or public tomb, where the war dead were buried. In the same area, many family plots have come to light.

C. More important than the monuments, however, were the funeral rites practiced by the living. Correct treatment of the dead is a profound social obligation in most societies, and the Greeks were no different. Rituals were used to ease both the living and the dead through the painful separation of death and to avert the pollution associated with death.

D. The first stage of burial was the *prothesis*. This began with the washing of the body, after which it was laid out. Inscriptional evidence suggests that the body was dressed in new clothes and laid on a mattress and coverlet specially purchased for the burial procession.

1. Geometric amphorae from about 750 B.C. depict scenes of the *prothesis*.
2. Mourners can be seen weeping and tearing their hair.
3. The body appears to be lying under a *baldacchino*.

E. The second stage was the *ekphora*. This was the procession escorting the funeral bier to the place of interment. Legislation limiting the amount of mourning and the number of attendants involved suggests that even before Pericles's time, the funeral procession had become noisy, costly, and disruptive.

1. These processions are also shown on the Dipylon vases from Athens.
2. The processions were led by armed men. Female family members walked close to the corpse, with other women following behind.

F. The final stage was the burial of the body or, in the case of cremation, the deposition of ashes. We are less well informed about this. For example, we do not know what formal words or prayers were said over the grave. In the offering trenches cut along some classical burials, the remains of animals, birds, and shells suggest that a meal may have been left for the dead.

1. The meal may have been burned as a sacrifice to the dead. The remains are often found with carbonized wood.

2. Literary sources often refer to libations poured for the dead. Wine was probably used, perhaps being poured on the ashes of the smoldering sacrificial meal.

III. The treatment of heroes was altogether different. Heroes were often associated with the founding or saving of the city or a colony.

   A. Heroes, and some heroines, received cult offerings at their tombs, which were often located at strategically important points: by the walls of the city, in the town square, or on the outer edges of the state's territory. Such a tomb was often a chamber covered by a mound.

   B. Heroes might receive sacrifices in the form of animals butchered and burnt, but more common was a blood sacrifice.

      1. At some hero shrines, a terracotta tube was built into the mound from the top to the chamber and was used to allow mourners to pour a libation into the tomb.

      2. Heroes, like other dead spirits, were thought to feed on blood.

   C. The Athenians of Pericles's day honored the 10 eponymous heroes who gave their names to the tribes of Athens. In addition, Theseus was regarded as the special founder hero of Athens. His importance grew as the power of Athens grew, and he served as an Athenian answer to the major Peloponnesian hero, Heracles.

      1. Athenian monuments, such as the Athenian Treasury at Delphi, showed both the labors of Heracles and the deeds of Theseus.

      2. A generation before Pericles, Cimon enhanced his own reputation and that of Athens by bringing the bones of Theseus back to Athens from Scyros.

   D. Many of the tombs where heroes were worshipped were actually Bronze Age or earlier tombs that had been disturbed. The Greeks were able to combine the hero saga of myth with the physical remains of earlier "heroic" society to establish holy and powerful markers in the landscape.

Suggested Reading:

Garland, R. *The Greek Way of Death*. Ithaca: Cornell University Press, 1985.

Antonaccio, C. *An Archaeology of Ancestors*. Lanham, MD: Rowman and Littlefield, 1994.

Questions to Consider:

1. Do the practices of the Greeks regarding death resemble those of modern societies in any way?
2. Why did heroes play so vital a role in the religious life of the Greeks?

Lecture Twelve—Transcript

Multiple Spouses and Matrilineality

In this lecture, we return to the Trobriand Islands, a chain of islands 150 miles off the coast of New Guinea that were made famous by Bronislaw Malinowski; you remember he worked there in the early 20th century, Malinowski, one of the earliest founders of anthropology and one of the big advocates of doing long-term fieldwork. Malinowski was there from 1914 to 1917, and the Trobriand Islands, based largely on his work, have become a classic case study in anthropology, and rightly so, given the richness of their cultural patterns. Indeed, on the Trobriand Islands we find ample illustrations of a number of topics that we've talked about in this class so far: the role of language; the importance of cultural models and magic and religion; and the crucial role played by kinship.

We have not just the work of Bronislaw Malinowski but also the anthropologist Annette Weiner, who worked in the Trobriand Islands in 1971 and 1972 and actually made a number of short trips back in the 1970s and 1980s. Weiner, as a woman, is able to provide us with a different perspective on Trobriand society. Malinowski had more access to the men—he spent more time with the men. There may have been a bit of sexist bias built into his work, understandable, given the age in which he worked, but Weiner had unique access to the female society in the Trobrianders, which really complements what Malinowski had to say.

The Trobriands are flat coral reefs, covered in very rich soils. The subsistence bases of the Trobriand Islanders are growing yams, taro, tobacco, and other crops, as well as fishing. Both Malinowski and Weiner worked on the largest and most important island in the Trobriand chain, which is the island of Kiriwina. Kiriwina has a population of about 12,000 and that's divided among more or less 60 villages, so a fairly dense population, about 200 people per village. Each of the villages on the Trobriand Islands are composed of groupings of houses, hamlets, and each village will have six, seven, or eight of these hamlets in a village. The hamlets are composed of houses, and the Trobrianders have these log houses that are built off the ground with very steeply arched thatch roofs, and in front of the houses are yam huts or yam houses, and these are often more elaborate than the main house.

Yams, and we're going to talk about yams in the Trobriand Islands later in the course, but yams are not only important staple items of the Trobriand diet but really important symbolic items in Trobriand cosmology. They symbolize a man's wealth. The chief's house, for example, will have a huge yam hut out front that will be filled with yams to show the world his wealth. Trobrianders speak variants of the language Kilivila; they also very often speak a neo-Melanesian pigeon language, and, interestingly enough, they have different languages for gardening. They have a different language for garden magic, and this is a language that has different words, different pronunciation, even a different rhythm to their speak. But what we know most, what we remember most about the Trobriand Islanders, is the fact that they are a matrilineal society; descent is traced through female lines, and, as we mentioned last time, in a matrilineal society children feel related to their mother and their mother's brother and their mother's sister as well in a way that they don't feel related to their father, much less their father's brother or their father's sister.

The Trobriand Islanders are a chiefdom. They have chiefs; chiefdomship is hereditary. They have lineages and clans, and these are ranked, some are ranked higher than others, but women are not the chiefs, only men, and men will inherit their position not from their fathers but from their mother's brother, their matrilineal male relative on the matrilineal side. A young man will inherit his position in society from his mother's brother. Likewise, a father will not pass on his position in society to his own biological son but rather to his sister's son. In Trobriand society, there's a great deference paid to chiefs. One is not supposed to make eye contact with chiefs, commoners always sit lower than chiefs, and there's this rigidity of contact between chiefs and commoners.

A number of things are passed down matrilineal in Trobriand society. Magic spells, for example, are passed down from men to their sisters' children, their sisters' sons. Each of the hamlets in a Trobriand village is a matrilineage, although not in practice. Not everyone who should live in a hamlet does—it depends on their particular circumstances—but everyone would maintain close contact to their home hamlet. Ancestral names are given by the mother's side of the family. It's a matrilineal society; they're named by the mother's side of the family but fathers also give names to their children, and this is significant. A father will ask his sister to give him a name to bestow upon his biological child, and this is the name that's most commonly used in everyday life, comes from the biological father.

Fathers also in Trobriand society give their children certain crucial adornments to wear, especially shell necklaces, these cowry shell necklaces. It makes the child look nice and also acknowledges paternity, and it also reflects on the social standing of the father. If he can afford to give his child really nice adornments to wear, it reflects well on him. As Annette Weiner pointed out, Malinowski got it a bit wrong when he described the relationship between fathers and their sons, and their children. Malinowski said that fathers and sons don't have anything to do with each other; they're like strangers. But Weiner says that actually fathers play a very important role. They give these adornments, they give these names; it's just not as important as mother's brother.

The key relationship in a matrilineal society is not between a husband and a wife; it is between brothers and sisters. This forms really the core of matrilineal society. A brother is related to his sister in a way in which he's not related to his own wife, a way that he's not related to his own children. His own children are not going to be members of his matrilineage, not going to be members of his family, but his sister's children will be members of his family. This very often leads to a joking relationship. This seems paradoxical to us, but fathers often have a joking relationship with their children, whereas what we would call uncle, mother's brother, has this strict authoritarian relationship, so fathers have more of what we would call in English an avuncular relationship, an unclety relationship with their children.

Let me mention here the origin myth that Trobrianders tell. The Trobrianders believe that in the beginning of all time, the primordial times, there was a society underground. There were Trobriand villagers, there were yam fields, there were chiefs. Everything that exists in Trobriand society today existed underground in this mythical world, and in the beginning of time brother and sister pairs came up through a hole from the underworld up onto the current earth. When they came up, they came up in pairs, and the first pair came up, and then the second pair came up, and then another pair, and all in all four brother-sister pairs came up from the underworld, and each of these was associated with a particular animal. There were the pigs, the dogs, the iguanas, and the crocodiles, so in Trobriand society today you have four clans, four people who trace their relationships back to a mythical ancestor, these mythical brother-and-sister pairs who came up from the underworld, and all Trobrianders are a member of one of these four clans.

They're named the pigs, the dogs, the iguanas, and the crocodiles, and these clans are ranked. The pigs came up first, then the dogs, and then the iguanas, and then the crocodiles, and everyone is born as a member of one of these clans in Trobriand society today. In the Trobriands, everybody has to marry outside of their clan, but one doesn't want to marry too far down. These clans are ranked: the pigs are first, the dogs are second, the iguanas are third, and the crocodiles are ranked last. Everybody has to marry outside of their own clan, but they don't want to marry too far down, so a pig wouldn't want to marry an iguana. A pig would want to marry someone from a dog clan, and so there's clan exogamy, but you don't want to marry too far down.

In many societies around the world—I want to talk about Trobriand marriage, but let me preface it with the general note—in many societies around the world, the preferred marriage partner is one's cross-cousin. In anthropology, we have two different terms for cousins, cross-cousins and parallel cousins. Cross-cousins are children of opposite sex siblings. This means that your mother's brother's children would be your cross-cousins, and your father's sister's children would be your cross-cousins. Parallel cousins, on the other hand, are children of same sex sibling, and so your mother's sister's children would be your parallel cousins and your father's brother's children would be parallel cousins. In many societies around the world, including the Trobrianders, these are two very different types of relatives. They're not all cousins, cross-cousins and parallel cousins. Many societies consider parallel cousins to be like brothers and sisters, and very often they'll use the term brother and sister to refer to parallel cousins, and in a number of cultures, like the Trobrianders, the preferred marriage partner is one's cross-cousin.

In the Trobrianders, there are four clans, and each person must marry outside of the clan; to marry inside of the clan is considered to be incestuous. Malinowski reported that the preferred marriage partner for men is the father's sister's daughter, cross-cousin; father's sister's daughter would be the preferred marriage partner for a man. This is neat because the father's sister's daughter is always going to be a member of a different lineage and clan. Remember that the children, your father is a member of a different matrilineage. The father's sister would be a member of that same matrilineage, and father's sister's children would be a member of that matrilineage, so it's marrying outside of one's lineage and outside of one's clan, but not marrying too far way. There are already relationships between those families, and so it's marrying outside of one's clan, but keeping the two clans held together, their interests being intertwined.

Malinowski said that children have to marry their father's sister's daughter, sons do, boys do. Weiner said actually that's not the case. That's the preferred form of marriage, this is what people would like to do in an ideal world, but in fact people very often—you know, your father's sister might not have gotten married; your father might not have a sister, the children might not be the right age; you might not like your cross-cousins. A multitude of factors could come into play here, and so people very often don't marry their father's sister's daughter; sons don't marry their father's sister's daughter, so there's some flexibility at play here.

Yams, as I've mentioned, are at the heart of Trobriand culture. It's a staple of the diet, but it's also the symbol of wealth and prosperity. In terms of marriage it's significant, because in the early days of marriage, for the first year of marriage, a couple will live together and the husband's mother will cook their food, will cook their yams, and bring it to their house, and this is like a probationary period for the marriage. And if the marriage lasts a year, the wife will set up a hearth in their own home and start cooking the yams, and when she cooks the first meal of the yams for her husband, this means that the marriage is going to last, it's going to solidify.

Trobriand men can marry several different women; they have a polygynous society, and this is very useful for Trobriand men because if they have aspirations of a noble lineage, of a chiefly lineage, if they have aspirations to build up their political power, by marrying different women they can make kinship alliances with various families. Economically, it's helpful to men to have more than one wife because there are more people in the household, more women in the household to help tend the gardens, to produce children, to help take care of the children and so forth, so polygyny is really a sign of wealth. It's a public symbol of being a powerful person. But the Trobriand husbands, just like Fulbe husbands, they can have more than one wife, but they have to support all of those wives in appropriate fashion.

Weiner paints a Margaret Mead-like picture of Trobriand life in which there's a lot of sexual experimentation going on among adolescents. The parents aren't very controlling. Couples go off into the forest and have trysts in the jungle, and there are all these little signs that adolescents will use to show that they're having relationships with someone else. A woman will bite off her lover's eyelashes, for example—I guess this is the equivalent of a hickey in our own culture. Over time, this period of experimentation often flowers into romantic love. That young girl and boy will go off with each other repeatedly, and eventually they may fall in love and get married. If they're not cross-cousins, the parents may allow it anyway because they want to indulge their children, and so romantic love comes into play as much as arranged marriage. There's also a very rich tradition of love magic in Trobriand society.

I want to talk a little bit about what happens after marriage in the familial relationships in a matrilineal society. A chief in Trobriand society is going to inherit his position from his mother's brother. Men get their position in life from their mother's brother, so it's inheritance through the female lines, but it's men who occupy these positions. How do ranks get established in the family? One gets chosen. The best analogy is English nobility. They would still have a basically high rank if they're from a chiefly family, but then there's a lot of negotiation, a lot of jockeying for power for people who can move up these ranks. You have to be born into a noble lineage, but then you can move up.

What's interesting about Trobriand society is that it's matrilineal, and it has what we call avunculocal residence, from avuncular, uncle, and local, so, ideally, a woman when she marries a Trobriand man goes to live with him, and they will both live with the husband's mother's brother, his uncle, avuncular residence, so a couple will go live with the husband's mother's brother. Again, this is an ideal rule, but in practice it doesn't always happen. If the boy is scheduled to inherit a position, a chiefly rank from his mother's brother, they always go and live with the mother's brother. In fact, there's a lot of play going on here where people can live elsewhere. Generally, boys who were destined to become their chiefs will go at age seven, eight, or nine years old. They'll move out from their father's household and go and move in with their mother's brother.

This leads to an unusual situation concerning the Oedipus complex in the Trobriand Islands. Property and status are inherited from a mother's brother in Trobriand society. Men exert control over their sister's sons like a father would. In a nutshell, as you're all familiar, just to remind you, the Oedipus complex argues that young boys, their first sexual attraction is toward their mothers, but they realize that mothers are the sexual property of their fathers, and so there's a conflict that goes on between boys and their fathers over sexual access to the mother. Malinowski, writing against Freud, said that in Trobriand society, the conflict that we find is not between fathers and their biological sons but between boys and their mother's brother, and so Malinowski said Freud got it wrong. Yes, there are these tensions between fathers and sons in Western society, but it's not about sex—it's about authority—and the authority figure is going to be resisted, and in Trobriand society, the father figure, the authority figure, is the mother's brother, and so that is who is resisted.

The Trobrianders have elaborate ceremonies that go on after the death of an individual. These are called *lisaladabu*, which literally means releasing emotional energy, and it's releasing the emotional energy which surrounds death. Women are considered to be the custodians of this emotional energy, and it's their responsibility to discharge it. In the death rituals, in the mortuary rituals, funeral rituals of the Trobriand Islanders, they divide up relatives of the dead person, and I'm going to speak about it today as if it were a man, the dead man, into two groups. There are the owners and the workers. The owners are the dead man's matriclan, the dead man's real family, his matriclan. The workers are the dead man's wife's family, the dead man's wife's matriclan, and the dead man's father's matriclan, so it's relatives. The affinal relatives are the workers, and the consanguineal, the blood relatives, the matrilineally related relatives, are the owners.

I'm going to come back to this in just a moment, but let me mention here that no death in Trobriand society is accidental, no death is accidental. There are no deaths by natural causes; they don't have a cultural model of dying from natural causes. It all comes from sorcery. There's always magic and sorcery involved. People don't die of disease; the disease concept of illness and death really doesn't exist. If you don't like somebody, if you're envious of somebody, if you have hard feelings, you can actually kill that person. This comes into play into this distinction between owners and workers at the death ceremony. The workers have to show that they didn't want the dead person killed. They're not of the dead man's family—they're his affinal kin; they're his in-laws, if you will—and since they're members of another competing lineage, they're automatically suspect of the death of an individual.

Did you not like this person? Did you think that they were taking resources from your lineage? The workers have to show the owners, the members of the dead man's matrilineage, that they're innocent of this death, and that they're truly sorry that the dead man died. The workers bring gifts: they'll bring stone axes; they'll bring betel nuts, this nut that Trobriand Islanders chew that's a mild stimulant, widely chewed in the South Pacific. They'll bring small gifts to give to the owners, and with these gifts they're saying "We didn't want this person to die; we're as sorry as you are that this person died. We didn't do the sorcery. We didn't make this person die," and they go through all of these ritualized wailings at certain times of the day. They'll scream as a group to indicate how sorry they are for the death that has occurred.

On the other hand, the members of the dead man's matrilineage, the owners of the body are not allowed to touch the body. They're only allowed to participate in certain ways in the funeral rituals; they're not allowed to have anything to do with the preparation of the body itself. They can't dress the dead man, they can't paint the person, all of the things that would go in for getting a body ready for burial. The owners can't get involved because that would pollute them, and so the workers have to do all of the work in the funeral ceremony. They have to get the body ready and go through all of the physical preparations that actually involves touching the body.

Some months after the burial and the funeral ceremony, there is a series of gift exchanges that occur, and what happens is the owners distribute gifts to the workers to compensate them, so let's go over what happens here. A man dies, the owners, his matrilineage, can't touch the body and they suspect his other kin, his wife's matrilineages and his father's matrilineage, of committing sorcery. Those kin, the workers, have to prove that they haven't done anything, and so they do all of the work, all of the preparation, and give gifts to the owners to show how sorry they are for this death, and then some months after the funeral ceremony the owners of the body will then give gifts back to the workers. They've accepted their explanation that they weren't involved in the death, so they give gifts back, and a lot of this involves women's wealth, which on the Trobriand Islands yams are men's wealth, and women's wealth are grass skirts made out of banana leaf bundles, very beautiful dyed grass skirts, and the women owners will give these to the workers to compensate them for all that they did. There's also some exchange of men's wealth, yams and so forth, but it's really the women's wealth that goes on in these final exchanges.

These mortuary ceremonies are very closely tied with the Trobriand notions of spirituality. They believe that every person has a spirit, and this is called *baloma*. A person's spirit, what we would call the soul, at death the soul doesn't die, but it goes off to a mythical island that they call Tuma. When a person dies, the soul, the spirit, *baloma*, goes off to Tuma, and there it gets old again and goes through a whole life cycle on this mythical island of Tuma, and when the spirit gets old and dies, it comes back to the Trobriand Islands, enters a woman's body and gets reborn as a fetus and as a member of the same matrilineage of the person who died, so from death is rebirth of the matrilineage. It's a cycle they keeps going on and on and is reborn again and again, so they literally see death as being crucial to the rebirth of their culture, not just a spiritual rebirth, but actual rebirth.

Famously, Malinowski said that the Trobrianders believe that a woman, that they didn't have a clear biological notion of procreation, and that the Trobrianders believe that a woman got pregnant by wading into the water and when she waded into the water, these spirits, these baloma would enter her body, and she would become pregnant. Malinowski pointed out that they noted that sex was required, but this was sex to build up seminal fluids in the woman's body, to form the bones and the brain and so forth. Weiner points out that these days lots of Trobrianders share our biological notion of where babies come from, but they continue to practice this idea of what Malinowski euphemistically called copulatory vigilance, and it means that having sex one time isn't enough for the fetus to grow, that a couple must have sex repeatedly in order to build up semen in the woman's body to form the brain and the bones and the other crucial parts of the body, and these are cultural models of biology, cultural models that we talked about last time that don't have to correspond exactly with what we will call the object of truth.

All of this ties into kinship, because when a person dies that person's spirit is also a future member of their lineage. You have all these rituals around you. With the burial ceremony, there are the workers who have to do the work, the owners who own the body and cannot work, and the workers have to show that they were not responsible for the death of the body and that they didn't want this to happen, and this is all made necessary because no death is accidental. All death is caused by sorcery; not even death by old age is considered to be accidental.

We have the Trobrianders, and they illustrate a number of points that we've made in this class. They illustrate the role of cultural models, cultural models of folk biology, the way in which people get pregnant, for example, cultural models of death, that the spirits cause death. The Trobriand Islanders also illustrate the role of kinship in a matrilineal society, this complex relationship of a child to his or her father, not what we would consider to be a natural relationship of a child to their father, but for the Trobrianders very natural, and the relationship of children to their mother's brother, who is the authority figure in this society, and this makes sense because a man's sister's children are going to be the ones who are going to carry on his lineage. They're going to be the ones who reflect on him when they grow up, so it's very important that he be the authority figure in their lives, and so children have a joking relationship with their biological fathers, and they have this authority, this more of a parent-child, what we consider to be a parent-child relationship with their mother's brother.

The Trobrianders illustrate our earlier discussions of cultural models. They illustrate our discussions of magic, their practice of love magic, of garden magic, their fear of illness and death through sorcery, and while Weiner critiqued Malinowski for underplaying the role of women in Trobriand society, together their work really gives us an incredibly rich picture of this fascinating place, and we will have an opportunity to come back and discuss the Trobrianders in later lectures.

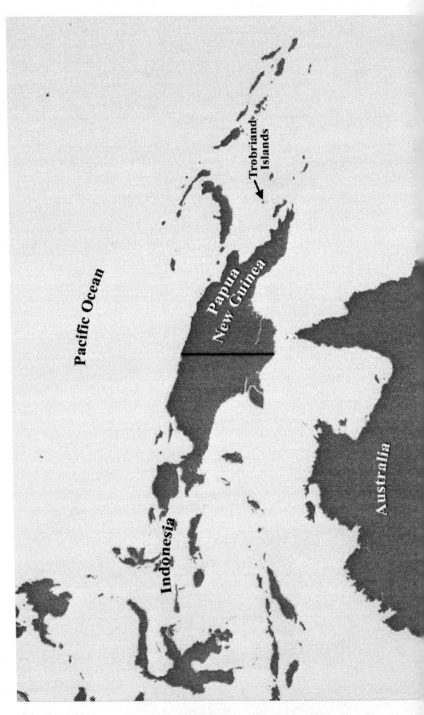

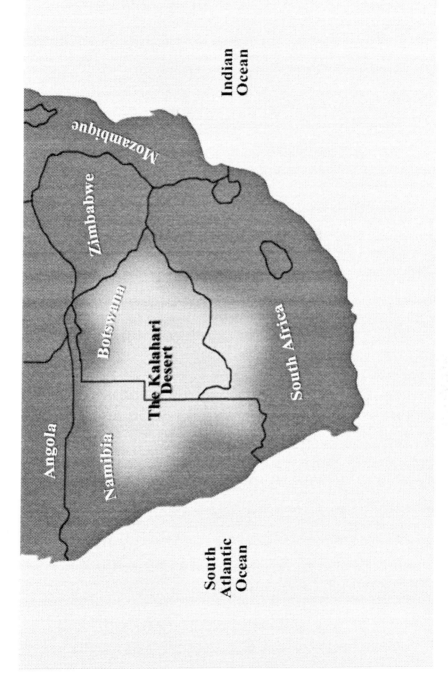

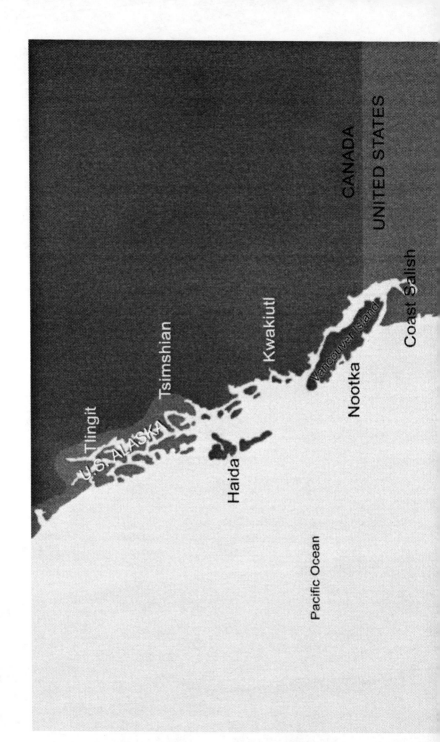

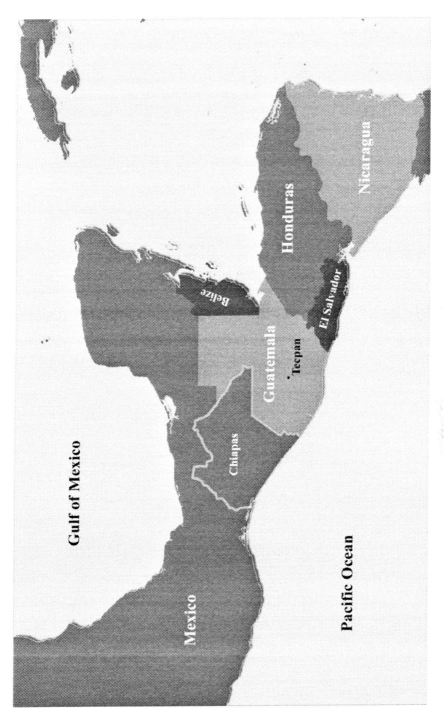

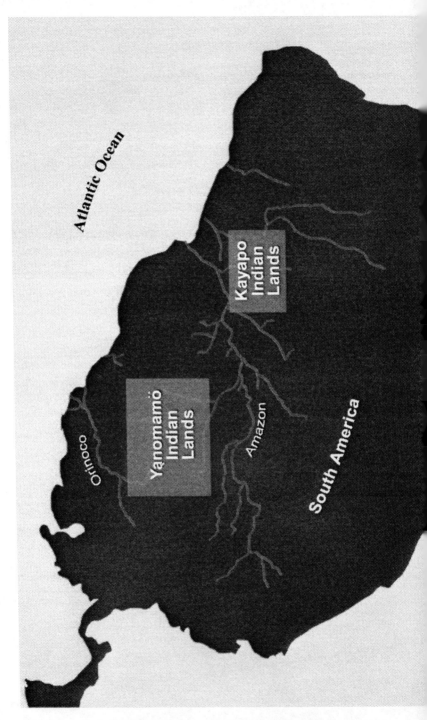

Cultural Sketches
(Biographical Notes)

Dobe Ju/'hoansi

The Dobe Ju/'hoansi are a hunting and gathering group living in small bands on the northwest edge of the Kalahari Desert in Botswana and Namibia. The Ju/'hoansi follow game and harvest cycles throughout the year, staying within areas defined by water holes. Their camps (which consist of grass huts set around an open plaza) are usually occupied for only a few months.

The Ju/'hoansi (who are also known as the Kalahari Bushmen, the San, and the !Kung) are a classic band-level society (as illustrated in Lecture Thirteen). They have are no formal positions of political authority, relying instead on situational leadership. Although we often think of hunters and gatherers as impoverished, studies have shown that there is actually very little hunger among the Ju/'hoansi and that the average workweek is only about 20 hours. In addition, the vast majority of their calories come not from meat but from gathered foods. The Ju/'hoansi also have little notion of private property and practice a generalized form of reciprocity (see Lecture Sixteen).

The Dobe Ju/'hoansi are one of the most thoroughly documented societies in the world, thanks to the work of Richard Lee, Irven DeVore, Marjorie Shostak, and others who worked on the Harvard Kalahari Project starting in 1963.

The Ju/'hoansi speak a San (or "click") language (discussed in Lecture Six). The / represents a dental click, a sound not unlike "tsk," as in a scolding ("tsk, tsk"). The *J* is pronounced as in the French "je." An alternate spelling is Zhu/wansi.

Fulbe

The Fulbe (also known as the Fulani) are an ethnic group spread out across West Africa. Numbering as many as 10 million people, the Fulbe all speak varieties of the Fulfulde language and are (at least nominally) Muslim. They trace their dispersed origins back to early 19th-century *jihads* that spread the faith westward across Africa.

Traditionally, they have had a chiefdom-style political organization, although sustained contact with colonial powers and modern African states has diminished the importance and power of chiefs. Most Fulbe are cattle herders, although the Fulbe of northern Cameroon studied by Helen Regis are farmers.

As discussed in Lecture Nine, the Fulbe have melded Islamic teachings with traditional beliefs. Koranic scholars (*Mallums*) are called upon to interpret scripture and to heal illnesses brought about by cannibal witch attacks and soul-stealing river spirits. There is a strict division between women and men in Fulbe life, but women have more power than in many other Islamic societies. They may divorce, for example, if their husbands do not adequately provide for them with annual gifts of batik cloth. The Fulbe also highly value stoicism; their code of conduct (*pulaaku*) calls for strong emotions to be muted.

The Fulbe also practice an important rite of passage for males (see Lecture Ten). Boys are taken to a temporary camp, where they are forced to eat unclean foods and learn secrets associated with manhood. They are then circumcised and return to the village as men.

Kwakiutl

The Kwakiutl are one of a number of related ethno-linguistic groups living along the northwest coast of North America, from British Columbia up to the Inuit territories of the sub-Arctic. The Kwakiutl were made famous by Franz Boas and his extensive studies of almost all aspects of native life, from language and arts to history and body measurements (see Lecture Three). The Kwakiutl and other northwest-coast groups are also known for their totem poles and spectacular masks (such as those in the collections of the American Museum of Natural History and the Chicago Field Museum).

Kwakiutl subsistence is based around salmon, which are seasonally abundant and can be dried for eating year-round. The Kwakiutl have a matrilineal society with a chiefdom style of political organization. Kwakiutl chiefs compete with one another to build their power through potlatch feasts (see Lecture Seventeen). During potlatch feasts, which would last for several days, hosts ply their guests with food and gifts. In addition, there are displays of conspicuous destruction—with canoes, artwork, and blankets sunk or burned. Potlatches were incredibly costly, and chiefs would often have to save for years to throw one, but a successful potlatch would secure valuable political allegiances. Some have argued that the potlatch also served as a form of insurance—if the salmon did not run one year, neighboring chief's potlatches could provide needed food and supplies. Potlatches were banned in Canada for many years as irrational acts of destruction. Recently, they have been revived by a new generation of Kwakiutl reclaiming their heritage.

Maya

When one thinks of the Maya, the first images to come to mind are likely of Classic-era Maya civilization (A.D. 250–900) that flourished in the lowland forests of Central America. Yet there are more than 6 million Maya people living today in southern Mexico, Guatemala, Belize, and Honduras. In Guatemala, the Maya make up over half of the population.

The Maya of Guatemala are concentrated in the thousands of small, rural communities spread throughout the western highlands. Because of rugged terrain and social isolation, this is an area of great linguistic diversity; 21 separate Mayan languages are spoken in Guatemala alone. Just as Spanish is the *lingua franca* of Guatemala, Catholicism is the common religion, but here, too, we find significant variation. Native shamans still maintain sacred ancient calendars and perform rituals, and Protestant missions are making significant inroads.

The vast majority of Maya in Guatemala are subsistence farmers, growing the staple crops of corn and beans. Guatemala is a country of stark inequalities, and the Maya suffer disproportionately from lack of land and poverty. During the late 1970s and early 1980s, they also suffered from military campaigns against communist guerrillas (a period known as *la violencia*). In Lecture Twenty-Two, I call on my fieldwork in the town of Tecpán Guatemala, to show the lasting impact of the violence on traditional lifeways.

It is easy to see the modern Maya as victims, but we must not lose sight of the fact that they take an active role in constructing their lives. Maya farmers around Tecpán, for example, have begun exporting snow peas and broccoli to the United States, using their traditional skills to increase their earnings by tapping into a global market. As we see in Lecture Twenty-Three, Maya activists in Guatemala and Mexico have also been successful in recent years in pushing for indigenous rights reforms.

Sambia

The Sambia are an Anga-speaking group in the New Guinea highlands. *Sambia* is a pseudonym used by Gilbert Herdt, the anthropologist who has worked with the Sambia since the late 1960s. Herdt used a pseudonym to protect the isolated Sambia from unwanted attention following the publication of his work.

The Sambia are a patrilineal chiefdom-level society. There is a stark division between men and women. Men view women as potentially polluting and try to keep contact to a minimum. Sambia houses have separate areas for men and women, and there are even separate male and female paths through their villages. Menstruating women are required to move out of their houses and into a menstrual hut located outside the village proper. Men, for their part, spend much of their early lives living in the village men's hut.

As discussed in Lecture Ten, the male initiation rites are the most dramatic aspect of Sambian society. The Sambia believe that males are not born with a supply of semen. Thus, to turn them into men, prepubescent boys are required to drink the semen of older boys. They learn this secret ritual through an intense initiation ceremony, after which they will live in the men's hut and practice ritualized homosexuality until they get married in their early 20s. After the birth of their first child, men are no longer supposed to have sexual contact with other males. Yet a fear of females as depleting a man's semen supply keeps men suspicious of their wives.

With increasing contact with the outside world (led by Seventh Day Adventist missionaries), the Sambia today are abandoning many of their former customs—moving into Western-style houses, going to church, and rarely conducting male initiations.

Trobrianders

The Trobrianders are a matrilineal chiefdom located on a string of small islands off the coast of Papua New Guinea. They were first studied by Bronislaw Malinowski during World War I (see Lecture

Four) and have since become a classic case study in cultural anthropology. Annette Weiner conducted an important restudy of the Trobrianders in the 1970s, focusing on a number of aspects of women's lives that Malinowski missed.

As discussed in Lecture Twelve, the Trobrianders are a matrilineal society with four ranked clans. Although descent is traced through female lines, men hold the formal positions of power (inherited from the mother's brother). Contrary to the expectations of Freud's Oedipal complex, adolescent Trobriand boys have tensions, not with their fathers, but with their mothers' brothers. Malinowski used these data to argue against the universality of the Oedipus conflict. Malinowski also wrote that a young man is obliged to marry his father's sister's daughter (a cross-cousin); Weiner found that although this may be a cultural ideal, in practice, men most often do not marry a cross-cousin. High-ranking Trobriand males often have several wives, which increases their kinship ties and political prestige.

A great deal of political maneuvering goes on between Trobriand chiefs jockeying for power. The material circumstances of chiefs are much as they are for everyone else—there is not much variation in standards of living. Wealth is more symbolic than material, and a key symbol of wealth and power is yams, displayed in yam huts in front of chiefs' houses. A full yam hut is a clear sign of political prestige; the catch is that these yams must be received as gifts. Men receive yams through their wives (from a wife's brothers, in particular). Weiner shows that this practice puts Trobriand men in debt to their wives, an obligation that must be repaid with women's wealth (banana-leaf bundles and woven skirts). For upwardly mobile chiefs, redistributions of yams serve as a means of building up political power (see Lecture Seventeen).

The Trobrianders are also known for the *kula* trade ring, an elaborate system of balanced reciprocity, as discussed in Lecture Sixteen. In the *kula* ring, men have trading partners on islands in either direction. To these partners, they trade armbands (which move only counter-clockwise through the ring) and necklaces (which travel only clockwise); both are made of shells, and each item has a particular history of ownership associated with it. To possess a famous item brings prestige, although the items are not hoarded and constantly circulate.

Yąnomamö

The Yąnomamö live in the rainforest at the border between Venezuela and Brazil. They number about 20,000, spread out over a large territory and living in villages called *shabonos* of between 40 and 300 people. They are best known from the long-term fieldwork of anthropologist Napoleon Chagnon, who worked primarily in the village of Bisaasi-teri in Venezuela.

In many ways, the Yąnomamö are a classic patrilineal tribal-level society (see Lecture Fourteen). Rather than hereditary chiefs, Yąnomamö *shabonos* have headmen who earn their positions through networking and leading by example. The Yąnomamö practice a slash-and-burn style of agriculture, growing plantains, manioc, taro, sweet potato, and tobacco. Using poison-tipped arrows, they also hunt pigs, monkey, deer, and armadillos.

The Yąnomamö live in a world filled with mischievous and malevolent spirits. Shamans use hallucinogenic snuff to contact and manipulate the spirit world. At death, the Yąnomamö cremate the bodies of their dead relatives, crush up the bones, and drink the mixture in a gruel—symbolically rejuvenating their lineage.

As discussed in Lecture Fifteen, the Yąnomamö are also an especially violent society, with frequent raids and warfare between *shabonos*. Men who have killed take on the status of *unokais* and generally have more wives than other men. Anthropologist Marvin Harris argues that the Yąnomamö fight because of chronic protein shortages, but Chagnon counters that, in fact, they are fighting over women.

The journalist Patrick Tierney has published a scathing critique of Chagnon's work with the Yąnomamö—accusing him of intentionally infecting the Yąnomamö with measles as part of a secret experiment. While the genocidal allegations have been disproved, Chagnon's work raises important questions about the impact of anthropologists (and the trade goods they bring with them) on native communities.

Glossary

achieved authority: political positions that must be earned through demonstrating one's worthiness (for example, headmen).

affine: a relative by marriage.

animism: a belief in souls.

ascribed authority: inherited political positions.

Australopithecine: early hominids (human ancestors) that walked upright, although they had relatively small brains.

balanced reciprocity: gift-giving with the expectation of receiving a counter-gift of comparable or better value.

bands: social groups of less than 50, without formal political positions, based on gathering and hunting economies; for example, the Dobe Ju/'hoansi.

berdache: third gender in North American Pueblo and Plains societies; men who dress and live as women.

bounded rationality: the idea that humans are more rational in certain contexts than in others.

chiefdoms: social groups with thousands of members, a political system based on hereditary authority; for example, the Trobrianders.

cognate: a word with the same root as the word under study.

cognitive models: mental models of how the world works; may be more or less idiosyncratic (personal models) or shared (cultural models).

communitas: the sense of community solidarity produced by collective passage through a state of liminality.

consanguine: a blood relative.

cross-cousin: children of opposite-sex siblings; one's cross-cousins would be one's father's sister's children and one's mother's brother's children.

cultural capital: a form of symbolic capital based on cultural competencies, including, for example, artistic knowledge and educational credentials.

cultural models: mental models of the world and how it works that are widely shared by members of a culture.

cultural relativism: the notion introduced by Boas that each culture should be considered on its own terms, rather than judged by the cultural standards of another.

ebene: the hallucinogenic snuff used by Yąnomamö shamans.

Erklärung: German, used by Max Weber to denote explanation and functional understanding, as opposed to the more subjective *Verstehen*.

emic: the view from within a culture; a cultural insider's explanations; contrast with etic.

endocannibalism: ritualized consumption of the remains of one's dead relatives.

endogamy: rule mandating marriage within a variably defined group (for example, marrying within one's religion or ethnic group).

environment of evolutionary adaptation (EEA): the early Pleistocene of East Africa, where human ancestors first evolved.

ethnocentrism: the (usually implicit) belief that one's culture is superior to others; that one's own cultural customs are "natural."

ethnography: the process of gathering data from fieldwork and writing it up; cultural descriptions of other societies.

etic: an outside perspective on cultural customs; contrast with emic.

exocannibalism: ritualized eating of one's enemies.

exogamy: rule of marriage outside a variably defined group; to marry within that group would be incest.

fa'fa'fines: third gender on Samoa; men who dress and live as women.

Fordism: mass production based on the assembly line model popularized by Henry Ford.

formalist economics: the study of universal laws of economics that are not bound by cultural context (compare with substantivist economics).

gender: the social category associated with a particular sex.

generalized reciprocity: in which gifts flow in one direction for long periods of time.

hau: the Maori concept of the spirit of a gift.

headman: political position in tribal-level societies; the headman must lead by example and constantly reaffirm his right to lead.

hegemony: as developed by Anotonio Gramsci, the notion that cultural forms can induce people to willingly accept subjugation and exploitation.

hekura: microscopic spirits that inhabit the Yąnomamö world; can steal one's soul; can also be manipulated by shamans.

historical particularism: the notion introduced by Boas that each culture is the product of its own unique history; opposed to the unilineal evolution of 19th-century theorists

hxaro **exchanges**: balanced-reciprocity exchanges practiced by the Dobe Ju/'hoansi, often involving glass beads and other trade goods.

hyperreality: term used by philosopher Jean Baudrillard to denote a copy that is, seemingly, more "real" than the original.

inclusive fitness: combines direct fitness (number of an individual's offspring that survive to reproduce themselves) with indirect fitness (the number of an individual's genes, carried by that person and his or her relatives, that are passed down to the next generation); used by sociobiologists to explain nepotism and altruism.

kinesics: the study of body language.

Ku: Hawaiian god of war.

kula: the exchanges of the Trobrianders, in which armbands and necklaces made from shells are traded through a large ring of islands.

late capitalism: stage of capitalist development that started in the 1970s and accelerated in the 1980s and 1990s; characterized by post-industrial knowledge and service economies, economic globalization, and post-Fordist production techniques.

liminality: concept introduced by Victor Turner to denote a temporary state in which normal social strictures are dropped; an inversion of normal social order associated with carnival and rites of passage.

Lono: Hawaiian god of fertility.

magic: belief that the supernatural world can be controlled through rituals; as compared to the belief in an omnipotent supreme being (religion).

milpa **agriculture**: maize and beans agriculture traditionally practiced by the Maya.

mwasawa: Trobriand period of "play" in the two months after harvest.

natural selection: the mechanism for evolution introduced by Darwin; certain variations among individuals may be favored by natural conditions.

negative reciprocity: taking advantage of the implicit expectations of gift-giving by accepting a gift but never reciprocating.

parallel cousins: cousins of same-sex siblings; one's mother's sister's children and one's father's brother's children.

phoneme: the minimal unit of sound; phonemes vary from culture to culture.

polyandry: marriage of one woman to more than one man.

polygyny: marriage of one man to more than one woman.

potlatch: feasts thrown by Kakiutl chiefs that involve massive redistribution, as well as conspicuous destruction.

post-Fordism: flexible production techniques adopted by Saturn and a number of other companies in the 1990s.

prisoner's dilemma: a foundational problem in experimental economics: two individuals are arrested for a crime they committed, but the police do not have enough evidence to convict them both of the crime. They are interrogated separately and each made the offer that if both refuse to confess, they will be convicted of a lesser charge and serve two years each; if both confess they will each serve four years; and if only one confesses, that person will go free while the accomplice will serve five years.

	Player B: cooperate	Player B: defect
Player A: cooperate	2 yrs./2 yrs.	5 yrs./0 yrs.
Player A: defect:	0 yrs/5 yrs.	4 yrs./4 yrs.

proxemics: the study of physical distance as a form of communication.

pulaaku: the Fulbe code of conduct that stresses stoicism.

Quetzalcoatl: a primary Aztec deity, usually represented as a feathered serpent, but also said to take the form of a light-skinned man (and, thus, perhaps initially confused with Cortes).

r and K selection: a species' reproductive strategies may be placed on a continuum from r (favoring a large absolute rate of reproduction—many offspring) to K (favoring a low rate of reproduction but investing heavily in those offspring).

Rashomon effect: from the 1950 Japanese film *Rashomon*, the effect of different observers perceiving the same event in very different ways.

sandbadham **marriage**: fluid marriages between Nayar (India) women and one or more "visiting husbands."

Sapir-Whorf hypothesis: the proposition that worldview and culture are at least partly dictated by grammar and language structure.

shabono: the Yąnomamö village made of a circular palisade, a thatched roof living area, and a large open plaza; may have between 40 and 300 inhabitants.

shaman: a religious specialist who acts as a mediator between the spirit world and the material world.

sim-pua **marriage**: a traditional Chinese form of infant betrothal.

social capital: networks of family, friends, and acquaintances that serve as important assets.

social Darwinism: line of thought developed by Herbert Spencer that attempted to apply Darwin's natural selection to human societies.

substantivist economics: the view than economic systems are culturally embedded, that there are no universal economic laws (compare with formalist economics).

swidden agriculture: also called slash-and-burn, the technique of cutting down and burning trees and vegetation on a plot before planting; swidden plots are usually farmed for several years, then a new plot is cut down.

symbolic capital: forms of non-material capital, such as social capital or cultural capital, that may be converted into material resources.

tali-**rite marriage**: a temporary and ceremonial marriage performed with young Nayar (India) girls, marking their passage into womanhood.

TAT: Thematic Apperception Test, a psychological test that shows subjects pen-and-ink drawings of various scenes and asks them to describe the scenes.

taupu: ceremonial virgins on Samoa, daughters of chiefs.

Taylorism: developed by Frederick Taylor, a method of production in which each process is broken down into its smallest components to reduce the need for skilled and artisanal labor.

Tenochtitlán: the Aztec capital city; today, the site of Mexico City.

traje: traditional Maya dress.

tribes: social groups with hundreds of members and a headman form of political authority, based on a horticultural economy; for example, the Yąnomamö.

ultimatum game: an experimental economics game that pairs two individuals. Player A is given a sum of money (x), a percentage of which he must offer Player B, who can either accept or reject the offer. If the offer is accepted, the money is split as offered, and if the offer is rejected, neither player gets any money.

unokais: honorific given to Yąnomamö men who have killed.

Verstehen: the German word used by Max Weber to denote a subjective understanding, as compared with the more functional *Erklärung*.

waiteri: the valued Yąnomamö personality quality of fierceness.

weapons of the weak: concept introduced by James Scott to denote the ways in which subjugated and disempowered peoples can exert resistance.

world systems theory: view of the global economy that sees less developed countries as dependent on more developed countries.

Bibliography

Films:

The Ax Fight. Timothy Asch and Napoleon Chagnon. Documentary Educational Resources, 1975. Multifaceted view of violent conflict between two Yąnomamö villages.

The Gods Must Be Crazy. Jamie Uys. Columbia TriStar, 1980. The fictional story of an isolated Kalahari band and their fateful encounter with a Coke bottle that falls from a passing airplane.

Books:

Appadurai, Arjun. *The Social Life of Things*. Cambridge University Press, 1988. Collection of essays examining the cultural biographies of commodities; see especially the essays by Appadurai and Kopytoff.

———. *Modernity at Large: Cultural Dimensions of Globalization*. Minneapolis: University of Minnesota Press, 1996. An anthropologist's account of the processes of cultural and economic globalization.

Barfield, Thomas. *The Dictionary of Anthropology*. Oxford: Blackwell Publishers, 1997. A useful basic source for definitions of terminology and concepts in anthropology.

Bass, Bill, and Jon Jefferson. *Death's Acre: Inside the Legendary Forensic Lab--the Body Farm--Where the Dead Do Tell Tales*. Putnam Publishing Group, 2003. A fascinating account of forensic anthropologist Bill Bass's work establishing the "Body Farm" at the University of Tennessee.

Baudrillard, Jean. *Simulation and Simulacra*. University of Michigan Press, 1995. Leading French philosopher's treatise on *simulacra* (copies with no original) and simulation in the modern economy; discusses hyperreality in the United States.

Benedict, Ruth. *Patterns of Culture*. Mariner Books, 1989. A seminal text written by one of Boas's early students. Benedict compares the Zuni, Kwakiutl, and other cultures in terms of core psychological traits.

Bestor, Theodore C. *Tsukiji: The Fish Market at the Center of the World*. Berkeley: University of California Press, 2004. An anthropologist looks at the world's largest fish market in Japan and the dense web of supply that keeps it stocked.

Boas, Franz. *Race, Language, and Culture*. University of Chicago Press, 1995. A collection of important articles written by the father of American anthropology in which he outlines his concept of cultural relativism by looking at race, language, and culture.

Bourdieu, Pierre. *Distinction: A Social Critique of the Judgment of Taste*. Harvard University Press, 1987. An important analysis of different forms of capital—not just economic but social and cultural as well—by one of France's leading contemporary theorists.

Brown, Michael. *The Search for Eve*. HarperCollins, 1990. Account of the recent research combining analysis of mitochondrial DNA with archaeological evidence to postulate a common human ancestor in East Africa about 200,000 years ago.

Burridge, Kenelm. *Mambu: A Melanesian Millennium*. Princeton, NJ: Princeton. University Press, 1995. Study of Melanesian cargo cults and millenarian religious beliefs in Melanesia.

Carmack, Robert. *Harvest of Violence*. Norman: University of Oklahoma Press, 1992. A collection of essays by anthropologists working in Guatemala on the effects of the violence in that country.

Chagnon, Napoleon. *The Yąnomamö*. International Thomson Publishing, 1992. Ethnography of the Yąnomamö of the Venezuelan rainforest.

Conklin, Beth. *Consuming Grief*. University of Texas Press, 2001. A moving account of death, grieving, and the practice of cannibalism among the Wari of the Brazilian Amazon.

Dawkins, Richard. *The Selfish Gene*. Oxford University Press, 1990. An important early text in sociobiology, arguing that humans are best seen, from an evolutionary perspective, not as individuals but as containers for selfish genes.

Diamond, Jared. *Guns, Germs and Steel*. New York: W.W. Norton & Company, 1998. Popular account of the rise of Western dominance.

Donner, Florinda. *Shabono*. San Francisco: HarperSanFrancisco, 1992. An impressionistic account of life among the Yąnomamö, focusing on spiritual beliefs and the roles of shamans.

Fagan, Brian. *People of the Earth: An Introduction to World Prehistory*. Prentice Hall, 2003. A comprehensive overview of archaeology and world prehistory.

Ferraro, Gary. *Classic Readings in Cultural Anthropology.* Wadsworth Publishing, 2004. A collection of seminal essays in cultural anthropology.

Fischer, Edward F. *Cultural Logics and Global Economies: Maya Identity in Thought and Practice.* Austin: University of Texas Press, 2001. Examination of economic and political globalization and their effects in a Maya community in Guatemala.

Fischer, Edward F., and R. McKenna Brown, eds. *Maya Cultural Activism in Guatemala.* University of Texas Press, 1997. Collection of essays examining the resurgence of Maya culture in Guatemala in the 1990s.

Fischer, Edward F., and Carol Hendrickson. *Tecpán Guatemala: A Modern Maya Town in Local and Global Context.* Westview Press, 2002. Ethnographic study of a Kaqchikel Maya town in highland Guatemala.

Fisher, Helen. *Anatomy of Love: A Natural History of Mating.* Ballantine Books, 1994. A biological perspective on human attraction and mating.

Friedman, Jonathan. *Cultural Identity and Global Process.* London: Sage Publications, 1994. Insightful essays on culture in an age of globalization.

Geertz, Clifford. *The Interpretation of Cultures.* Basic Books, 2000. A widely cited collection of essays on the meaning of culture; includes a classic analysis of the Balinese cockfight.

Goldstein, Melvyn C. "When Brothers Share a Wife." *Natural History*, March 1987, pp. 39–48. An analysis of fraternal polyandry among the ethnic Tibetans living in the Nepalese Himalayas.

Goody, Jack. *The Development of the Family and Marriage in Europe.* Cambridge University Press, 1983. A wide-ranging study of changing customs of marriage and the family in Europe of the last centuries; includes a detailed discussion of incest taboos as defined by the Catholic Church.

Gramsci, Antonio. *The Prison Notebooks.* Internal Publishers Company, 1971. Reflection on the concepts of hegemony, Fordism, and culture, written while the author was in prison in Italy.

Gregor, Thomas. *Anxious Pleasures.* University of Chicago Press, 1987. A study of the Mehinaku of the Brazilian Amazon, focusing on sexuality and psychology.

Gutman, Matthew. *The Romance of Democracy*. University of California Press, 2002. A sensitive ethnography looking at the complexities of democracy in a barrio of Mexico City.

Hall, Edward T. *The Silent Language*. Anchor, 1973. An analysis of language and nonverbal communication.

Harris, Marvin. *Cannibals and Kings: Origins of Culture*. New York: Random House, 1977. A lively materialist interpretation of a wide range of cultural traditions, from Aztec cannibalism to Muslim pork taboos.

Herdt, Gilbert. *Sambia Sexual Culture: Essays from the Field (Worlds of Desire)*. University of Chicago Press, 1999. Ethnographic study of the Sambia of Papua New Guinea, looking at their unusual sexual customs.

Jankowiak, William. *Sex, Death and Hierarchy*. Columbia University Press, 1992. Rich ethnographic account of life in an Inner Mongolian city.

Kearney, Michael. *Reconceptualizing the Peasantry*. Westview Press, 1996. A pioneering look at peasants in a globalized world. Calls on the author's fieldwork in Oaxaca, Mexico, and with Oaxacan immigrants to California.

Lakoff, George, and Johnson, Mark. *Metaphors We Live By*. University of Chicago Press, 2003. Linguistic analysis of key metaphors in American English.

Lee, Richard. *The Dobe Ju/'hoansi*. Harcourt Brace, 1993. Ethnographic study based on long-term fieldwork among the Dobe Ju/'hoansi of Botswana.

Lévi-Strauss, Claude. *The Raw and the Cooked*. University of Chicago Press, 1983. The first in a series of books that analyzes the structure of myths of native American groups.

Lizot, Jacques. *Tales of the Yanomami*. Cambridge University Press, 1991. Engaging study of Yąnomamö oral traditions and daily life.

Low, Setha. *Behind the Gates*. New York: Routledge, 2003. An ethnographic analysis of life in an American gated community.

Malinowski, Bronislaw. *Argonauts of the Western Pacific*. Waveland Press, 1984. Malinowski's study of the Trobriand Islanders, focusing on the *kula* ring.

———. *The Sexual Lives of Savages*. Routledge, 2001. Malinowski's account of kinship, marriage, and sexuality among the Trobriand Islanders.

Marcos, Subcomandante. *Our Words Are Our Weapons*. SevenStories Press, 2002. Writings from the poetic and charismatic leader of Mexico's Zapatista revolution.

Marx, Karl. *The Eighteenth Brumaire of Louis Bonaparte*. Internal Publishers Company, 1963. A biting critique of French peasants who supported Louis Bonaparte.

Mauss, Marcel. *The Gift*. W.W. Norton, 2000. Classic treatise on the nature of gift-giving.

Mead, Margaret. *Coming of Age in Samoa*. Perennia, 2001. Mead's best-selling account of the sexual lives of adolescent Samoan girls.

Menchu, Rigoberta. *I Rigoberta Menchu, an Indian Woman*. London: Verso Books, 1987. Nobel-prize winner's autobiographical account of life in Guatemala during the violence.

Mintz, Sidney. *Sweetness and Power: The Place of Sugar in Modern History*. New York: Penguin, 1990. A fascinating study of how demand for sugar in England influenced production on plantations in the New World.

Monetjo, Victor. *Testimonio: Death of a Guatemalan Village*. Curbstone Press, 1987. A moving account by a Maya anthropologist of the Guatemalan army's raid on the village where he taught school.

Morris, Desmond. *The Naked Ape*. Delta, 1999. An early sociolobiological perspective on humans as animals.

Murphy, Yolanda, and Robert Murphy. *Women of the Forest*. Columbia University Press, 1985. Sensitive portrait of gender relations among the Mudurucu of Brazil.

O'Connor, Geoffrey. *Amazon Journal*. Plume Books, 1998. A journalist's gripping account of social and environmental change in the Amazon region.

Pinker, Steven. *The Language Instinct*. Perennial, 2000. Provocative overview of recent research on language and the way the mind works. Pinker argues that language is a human instinct.

Rathje, William. *Rubbish! The Archaeology of Garbage*. Harper Perennial Library, 1993. An overview of Rathje's ongoing archaeological excavation of modern garbage dumps.

Regis, Helen. *The Fulbe of Northern Cameroon*. Westview Press, 2002. Ethnographic account of the Fulbe of northern Cameroon.

Remnick, David, ed. *The New Gilded Age*. New York: Random House, 2000. Insightful essays from the *New Yorker* on the culture of the 1990s economic boom.

Restall, Matthew. *Seven Myths of the Spanish Conquest*. Oxford University Press, 2003. This erudite and highly readable study debunks a number of common preconceptions about Spanish contact in the New World.

Sahlins, Marshall. *Stone Age Economics*. Aldine de Gruyter, 1972. Important text in which Sahlins argues that gathers and hunters are the "original affluent society," as well as an analysis of reciprocity across cultures.

————. *Islands of History*. University of Chicago Press, 1987. Sahlins's interpretation of the clash of cultures between Captain Cook and the Hawaiians, in which he attempts to solve the mystery of who killed Captain Cook.

Scheper-Hughes, Nancy. *Death without Weeping*. University of California Press, 1992. Moving account of life in an impoverished Brazilian shantytown.

————. *Saints, Scholars and Schizophrenics*. University of California Press, 2001. Psychological analysis of social life in a small community in western Ireland.

Schultz, Emily, and Robert Lavenda. *Cultural Anthropology*. McGraw-Hill Humanities/Social Sciences/Languages, 2000. Useful general introduction to cultural anthropology; a college textbook.

Scott, James. *Weapons of the Weak*. Yale University Press, 1987. A political scientist who has conducted fieldwork in Malaysia writes about the subtle ways in which disempowered individuals resist domination.

Shore, Bradd. *Culture in Mind*. Oxford University Press on Demand, 1996. Clear and well-written introduction to cognitive models.

Soshtak, Majorie. *Nisa: The Life and Words of a !Kung Woman*. Harvard University Press, 2000. The fascinating oral history of a Dobe Ju/'hoansi woman and the trials and tribulations she faces in love, marriage, and motherhood.

Stiglitz, Joseph E. *Globalization and Its Discontents*. W.W. Norton & Company, 2003. Nobel-prize winner's critique of economic globalization and misuses of economics.

Tannen, Deborah. *You Just Don't Understand: Women and Men in Conversation*. Quill, 2001. A sociolinguistic analysis of speech differences between men and women.

Thayer, Richard H. *The Winner's Curse: Paradoxes and Anomalies of Economic Life*. Princeton: Princeton University Press, 1994. A prominent economist explains irrational behaviors.

Tierney, Patrick. *Darkness in El Dorado*. New York: W.W. Norton & Company, 2002. An investigative journalist's scathing critique of Chagnon's fieldwork among the Yamomamö.

Turner, Victor. *The Ritual Process*. Aldine de Gruyter, 1995. Important contribution to the study of ritual that introduced the concepts of liminality and *communitas*.

Watson, James. *Golden Arches East*. Stanford, CA: Stanford University Press, 1997. A collection of essays looking at how McDonald's has been localized in Asian countries.

Weiner, Annette. *The Trobrianders of Papua New Guinea (Case Studies in Cultural Anthropology)*. International Thomson Publishing, 1988. Study of the Trobriand Islanders based on fieldwork in the 1970s; updates many of Malinowski's observations.

Whorf, Benjamin. *Language, Thought, and Reality*. MIT Press, 1964. Collection of essays outlining the Sapir-Whorf hypothesis.

Wilk, Richard. *Economies and Cultures*. Westview Press, 1996. A useful introduction to economic anthropology, covering both formal economics in the Adam Smith tradition and Marxist approaches.

Wilson, E. O. *On Human Nature*. Harvard University Press, 1988. Manifesto of a preeminent scholar of sociobiology.

Wolf, Arthur. *Sexual Attraction and Childhood Association*. Stanford University Press, 1995. Study of sexual attraction that supports the idea that sustained early childhood association mutes sexual desires. Field data from ethnic Chinese of Taiwan..

Wright, Robin. *The Moral Animal*. Vintage, 1995. A journalist's well-written synthesis of recent sociobiological work, focusing on the biological bases of morality.

Young, Michael. *Malinowski's Kiriwina*. Chicago: University of Chicago Press, 1998. Collection of photographs taken during Malinowski's fieldwork in the Trobriand Islands.

Internet Resources:

http://anthro.palomar.edu/tutorials The Anthropology Tutorials. Dr. Dennis O'Neil, Palomar College.

http://www.koko.org/. The Gorilla Foundation.